PRO FOOTBALL'S KICKING GAME

PRO FOOTBALL'S
KICKING GAME

George Sullivan

Illustrated with photographs and diagrams

DODD, MEAD & COMPANY

New York

PICTURE CREDITS

Vernon J. Biever, 25, 27, 28, 60; *Chicago Tribune*, 20; Collection of Mario Marciani, 21; Houston Oilers, 55; Miami Dolphins, 77; New York Public Library, 11, 12, 131; Pro Football Hall of Fame, 14, 15, 16, 17, 18, 23, 26, 125, 128, 133; San Diego Chargers, 98, 99. Jacket photograph in color by Bob Olen; Jim Bakken of the St. Louis Cardinals shows classic kicking form. All other photographs are by George Sullivan.

Frontispiece: **Dolphins' field-goal specialist Garo Yepremian tunes up in the shadow of Dick Anderson's high-stepping kick.**

Copyright © 1973 by George Sullivan
All rights reserved
No part of this book may be reproduced in any form without permission in writing from the publisher
ISBN: 0-396-06800-6
Library of Congress Catalog Card Number: 73-1653
Printed in the United States of America

To Midge, who hardly ever kicks

ACKNOWLEDGMENTS

Many persons contributed toward making this book possible. Special thanks are offered the following: Don Weiss, Director of Public Relations, and Joe Browne, National Football League; Jim Heffernan, Director of Information, National Football Conference; Don Smith, Director of Public Relations, Pro Football's Hall of Fame; Ed Croke, New York Giants; and Frank Ramos, New York Jets. Also helpful were: Charlie Callahan, Miami Dolphins; Jerry Wynn, San Diego Chargers; Pat Horne, New England Patriots; Jim Fox, New Jersey Jaycees; Herb Field Art Studio; George S. Halas, Jack Cusack, and Ken Strong.

CONTENTS

THEY CALLED IT *FOOT*BALL

Monday morning's headlines usually go to the quarterbacks and the running backs because they're the men who move the ball and are on the field the most. But place-kickers, punters, and the players who run back kicks (or try to prevent the opposition from running them back) are playing an increasingly important role.

No team can expect to reach the Super Bowl without having one man who is strong and deadly accurate as a place-kicker and another whose specialty it is to boom punts. The kicking game now decides one out of every three contests in the National Football League.

Kickers are the game's highest scorers. Look at the statistics for any recent year. Running backs don't even begin to make the list until you get down around fourteenth or fifteenth place.

Today's skilled kickers have made perfection commonplace. If Tom Seaver were ever to throw more than ten strikes in a row, it would make headlines. The finest basketball professionals miss at least one out of ten from the foul line. But when Jan Stenerud or Fred Cox lines up to try an extra point, fans take it for granted it will be good.

Through the 1972 season, forty-four-year-old George Blanda had 245 points-after in a row without a miss. Every decade or so he'd blow a couple. As for consistency on field goals, Garo Yepremian,

Tom Dempsey—63 yards!

10

in the first seven years of his career, didn't miss once from inside the 20-yard line.

Their efficiency from close up doesn't alone explain why kickers are becoming the game's dominant force. The first pro football game is said to have been played in 1895, and in all the ensuing years through 1969 no one kicked a ball more than 60 yards for a field goal. Tom Dempsey broke the barrier in 1970 by kicking a 63-yarder. Field goals of 50 yards and more, while not exactly common, are being booted with increasing frequency, but since Dempsey's feat they're hardly noticed.

Kickers have become so successful in so many ways, and have come to have such an enormous impact on the game, that within the next few years they may receive that ultimate of tributes—the rulesmakers will seek to repress them in some way.

Already people are talking about doing away with the extra point, reducing the value of the field goal, or moving the goal posts back to the end line. Something. Anything.

The first game of football in the United States was played between two colleges, Princeton and Rutgers, on November 6, 1869, at New Brunswick, New Jersey. It wasn't football as it's known today, but a modified version of soccer, or association football, with twenty-five men to a side. No running with the ball was permitted. It could only be advanced by the foot. Besides Rutgers and Prince-

Footwork was the leading feature of early football.

ton, "foot ball," as it was called, was played by Yale and Columbia.

But not Harvard. Harvard students preferred a game played with a big, egg-shaped ball, the rules of which were similar to those for rugby, a British game in which players on competing teams could (and can) kick, dribble, or run with the ball, but not pass it.

Eventually the other colleges became sold on the game Harvard played and when, on November 23, 1876, the Intercollegiate Football Association was formed, the directors adopted a set of rules that closely resembled those of English rugby. Since there was a decided emphasis on the kicking game in rugby, the same was true of early football. There were several types of kicks—the punt, the place kick, and the drop kick. In the last named, the kicker would drop the ball on its nose, then kick it the instant it rebounded.

A skilled drop-kicker was vital to a team's success. "A man . . . who devotes his time and attention to the thorough mastery of drop-kicking," said a contemporary source, "becomes not only a sought-after player, but also one who, more frequently than any other, has at his very feet the opportunity of securing victory for his side."

Drop kicks, place kicks, and punts were only a part of it. When teams of the 1880's faced one another across the line of scrimmage, the center, called the "snap-back" then, used his feet to put the ball in play. He didn't hand the ball back or pass it back as he does today. Walter Camp, often called "the father of American football," in an article he wrote in 1890, compared this aspect of the

Drop-kicking

game to rugby: "Our players began exactly as the Englishmen, by putting the ball on the ground, closing around it, and then kicking it until it rolled out somewhere. Soon an adventurous spirit discovered that he could so place his foot upon the ball that by pressing suddenly downwards and backwards with his toe, he could drag or snap the ball to the man behind him."

The way points were scored is further evidence of how important the foot used to be. A touchdown in the 1880's merely entitled the scoring team to a "try-at-goal"—a field-goal attempt; if the kick was good, the team was awarded six points. A missed kick was worth four consolation points. A field goal alone in those days earned five points.

Fundamental changes were made in the game before the century ended, and gradually football came to resemble rugby less and the game we know today more. The number of players was reduced from fifteen to eleven. The system of downs was established. Tackling below the waist was introduced in 1888.

Not all the changes improved the game. By the early 1900's, football was a brutal sport. The offense emphasized mass-momentum power plays. Defenses gang-tackled. Injuries were common and deaths were not rare.

Religious leaders, educators, and the newspapers began to call for the abolition of football. Theodore Roosevelt, an avid sportsman, who, as a football enthusiast and Harvard alumnus, had written a congratulatory letter to a Harvard fullback, thanking him for a victory over Yale, was President at the time. He wanted the game retained but he wanted an end put to the killing and maiming.

Roosevelt called to the White House several prominent members of football's rules committee. He told them of his concern and that unless they made changes in the game it might be outlawed.

Changes were made—right away. The most important one had to do with the forward pass. Previously the pass had been illegal and any attempt to throw the ball forward cost five penalty yards. Under the revamped rules, forward passing was permitted, an innovation that was to revolutionize the game.

Pro football was active during this period, but not very. It was played on the back lots and baseball diamonds of towns in Ohio and Pennsylvania. There were no leagues and little organization. Games were mostly pickup contests between college players hired for the day.

However, there were many outstanding professional players, and some of them were brilliant kickers. Jim Thorpe, for instance. When Thorpe became a pro player in 1915 by signing with the Canton Bulldogs, most of his best days were already in the record books. He was twenty-seven, yet his career in football was to continue for another ten years.

Thorpe first won fame for his all-around football skills as a college player at the United States Indian Industrial School at Carlisle, Pennsylvania, known simply as Carlisle Institute. He was one of

several fine kickers the team boasted. "Every man knew what to do with his toe," Carlisle coach Glenn S. (Pop) Warner once wrote. "Nowadays [1932] a team is lucky if there's one good leg in the lot, but it was nothing for Carlisle to have half a dozen."

Thorpe zoomed to international prominence in 1912 by winning gold medals in the Olympic pentathlon and decathlon competition, but later he was stripped of his titles because it was said he was not an amateur, that he had played professional baseball. The controversy has continued to the present day.

Jack Cusack was the man who signed Thorpe to his first pro football contract. When he agreed to pay Thorpe $250 a game, people said he was leading the Bulldogs into bankruptcy. But Thorpe proved to be a tremendous drawing card, and crowds at Canton home games doubled in size and then doubled again.

In his second game for the Bulldogs, Thorpe drop-kicked a field goal from the 18-yard line, then later in the game, from the 45-yard line, he place-kicked a field goal. The Bulldogs won, 6-0, a victory that enabled them to clinch the Ohio League title.

Thorpe could also raise havoc with his punting. One day during the season of 1920, Thorpe led the Bulldogs into Chicago for a meeting with the Bears. The field on which they played (now Wrigley Field) had end zones that sloped down and away from the goal posts. Whenever the Bears had to punt from their own end zone, George Halas, the team captain, would ask Thorpe for permission to come out of the end zone and kick. It was always okay with Thorpe. After the kick return, the ball was placed down so as to allow for the difference.

During the course of the game, the Bulldogs fumbled on third down in the shadow of their goal posts, on about their 5-yard line. A punting situation was at hand. Thorpe walked over to where Halas was standing and asked him if it would be all right, because of the downhill slant, to come out of the end zone to punt. It was the first time Jim had ever made the request, but Halas, tasting victory, said no.

Thorpe boiled. The team huddled briefly and then Jim stalked into the end zone to await the snap from center. When it came, he took two steps and then drove his powerful right leg into the ball, catapulting it downfield over the heads of the Chicago safetymen. After it hit down, it kept going and going. When it finally stopped, it rested on the Chicago 3-yard line.

"If Thorpe were playing today," said Cusack, a Texas oilman until his death in 1973, "he would be pro football's outstanding kicker. No question about it. Sixty yards was an average punt for him.

"He had enormous physical strength. That's

Pete (Fats) Henry held early punting and drop-kicking records.

15

what made him great. The ball spiraled off his foot, sometimes curving to the left, other times hooking right. Practice? He'd kick a few times before a game, but as for working out during the week, nobody did that. It was a different game then."

Sometimes Thorpe would tune up his leg by standing on one goal line and attempting to punt to the other. The man often posted at the opposite end of the field was teammate Pete (Fats) Henry, a 6-foot, 250-pound tackle. Like Thorpe, Henry was a spectacular kicker, and once held the NFL record for the longest punt—94 yards. In the Canton-Akron game of 1923, Henry drop-kicked a record 50-yard field goal. Two years later the record was equalled by John (Paddy) Driscoll, another of pro football's most noted kickers during the game's formative years.

Driscoll had been a high school star in Evanston, Illinois, and team captain at Northwestern University, then he entered the Navy. During 1919, as a kicker for the Great Lakes Naval Training Station, he booted a 30-yard field goal in the Rose Bowl and passed for a touchdown, as the Bluejackets defeated the Mare Island Marines, 17-9.

When Driscoll joined the Chicago Cardinals in 1920, the team's owner agreed to pay him $300 a game, a fantastic sum for the time. Driscoll showed he was worth it, however, especially whenever the Cards happened to be playing their cross-town

rivals, the Bears. During 1922 the teams faced each other twice. In their first meeting Driscoll drop-kicked two field goals; the Cards won, 6–0. On the second game Driscoll drop-kicked three, the Cards winning, 9–0. Year in, year out, it was much the same. Finally Bears' owner George Halas decided that there was only one way to solve the problem. He hired Driscoll away from the Cards.

Driscoll remained with the Bears for many years, as a player from 1926 to 1928, and later as coach

Paddy Driscoll

Ernie Nevers poses.

of the team. He was elected to Pro Football's Hall of Fame in 1965, one of the few kickers to be so honored. Recently Halas said that he "would have as great a feeling of security" in Driscoll's skill as a drop-kicker as he might have for any kicker of the present day.

The place-kicker was also very much a part of early pro football. The indomitable Ernie Nevers, one of the most fearsome running backs of all time, not only carried the ball but did the place-kicking for his teams, the Duluth Eskimos, and later, the Chicago Cardinals. On November 28, 1926, Nevers booted a record five field goals for the Eskimos in a game against the Hartford Blues. The record stood for forty years.

Despite the heroics of Nevers, Driscoll, Henry, and Thorpe, the kicking game was on a downhill slide. When Knute Rockne built his football powerhouses at Notre Dame during the 1920's, he did it on the basis of the forward pass, and the players who spearheaded the Irish attack were those who could throw the ball, catch it, or run with it. Kicking? It was all but forgotten, although Rockne did have some capable kickers. One was George Gipp, the legendary "Gipper," whose drop kicks won several games. Another was Frank Carideo, a punter. To coach Carideo, Rockne brought in LeRoy Mills, a well-known specialist of the day. Rockne himself didn't have the time.

Other noted coaches of the day, such as Glenn

S. (Pop) Warner and Howard Jones, both of whom made important and original contributions in the development of football offensive strategy, looked upon the kicking game in a negative fashion. Punting became purely a defensive weapon during this period, something to be used when everything else had failed. The place kick for a field goal came to be regarded as an admission of defeat. Only a team too weak to score a touchdown would think of trying one.

The rulesmakers continued to discriminate against the kicking game. In 1927 they decreed that the goal posts had to be set ten yards behind the goal line, a change which was meant to get posts out of the way of running backs and receivers. Previously the field goal had been reduced in value from five points to three.

The kicking game also suffered by virtue of what was happening to the ball, which was changing from a roundish object resembling the rugby ball—a ball that was meant to be kicked—to one that was slim and streamlined, obviously meant for throwing. The ball of the 1920's was 23 inches around the middle and difficult to grip. The girth was then reduced several times, and by 1934 it was down to 21½ inches. Anyone with a hand of no more than average size could grasp it firmly and throw it a good distance with accuracy. A person with long and strong fingers—someone like Slingin' Sammy Baugh of the Washington Red-

The "pumpkin ball" aided the cause of early kickers.

skins—could throw it 40 yards and more and hit the bull's-eye.

Kickers yearned for the pumpkin ball. Earl (Dutch) Clark, an All League quarterback with the Portsmouth (Ohio) Spartans in 1931 and later with the Detroit Lions, was also a gifted drop-kicker. Clark, known for his accuracy, was active in the game during the years the ball was being reduced in size. "The longer I played," he says, "the less accurate I became. The big ball was easy to kick. The trimmer one wasn't."

In Clark's final years in pro football, he place-kicked the ball instead of trying to drop-kick it. Other drop-kickers did the same or, better, learned how to throw it.

ENTER THE SPECIALIST

Charles Freeman Erb, a West Coast All American and later a coach, surveyed the state of the football world during the late 1930's and set down his observations in a treatise titled "The Lost Art of Kicking." But even as Mr. Erb was lamenting, the pendulum had already begun to swing the other way.

The people who had made it swing were owners of teams in the National Football League, which had been organized in 1920. Baseball and college football were *the* sports of the day and pro football had rough sledding. The Great Depression of the early 1930's made things even worse. In 1926 the fledgling league was made up of twenty-two teams; in 1932 only nine were in operation, most of the others having been engulfed in a great sea of red ink.

General economic conditions weren't the only problem. In February, 1933, when the club owners assembled for their annual meeting, George Halas, owner of the Chicago Bears, and George Marshall, who owned the Boston Redskins, warned their colleagues that they had to start putting on a more colorful show. As it was, they argued, pro football was often dull and drab. Their evidence was that 20 per cent of the games played the previous season had ended in ties, many of them scoreless ties. People didn't want to see tie games, Halas

declared. They wanted to see games played to a decision. They wanted scoring; they wanted action.

The other owners agreed. It was decided to tinker with the rules a bit to put some razzle-dazzle into the game. One of the rule changes that was proposed and approved permitted a forward pass to be thrown from any point behind the line of scrimmage. Previously, the passer had to be at least five yards behind the line. Many more passes were the immediate result.

Second, the owners agreed to move the goal posts back to where they had been planted originally—on the goal lines. This, they knew, would increase the number of field goals and make easier the scoring of points after touchdown.

Ironically, the two teams to most benefit from the rule revisions were Marshall's Redskins (who had switched to Washington) and Halas' Bears, the Redskins because in 1937 they acquired Sammy Baugh, one of the great passers of all time. The Bears didn't have to wait until 1937. On their roster at the time the rule change was made, they had young Jack Manders, fresh from the University of Minnesota. "Automatic Jack," as he was to be nicknamed, was to become pro football's leading place-kicker of the 1930's.

Beginning with the first game of his rookie season of 1933 until the third game in 1937, he established a pro record of 72 consecutive PATs with-

out a miss. In 1934 he set a season record for field goals with ten, a record that was to stand for almost twenty years.

Like kickers of the present day, Manders credited his holder, Carl Brumbaugh, with playing a vital role in his kicking success. The two went through an elaborate ritual before every kick. While Manders wiped off the toe of his kicking shoe, Brumbaugh constructed a small dirt tee for the ball about eight yards behind the line of scrimmage, then he would turn and spit on the toe of Manders' shoe. The pair insisted that all of this was very necessary. Perhaps it was. When, after almost four full seasons of perfection, Manders finally missed an extra-point try, someone other than Brumbaugh—a nonspitter, no doubt—was doing the holding.

"Place-kicking," Manders once said, "is a matter of timing, concentration, and practice. A kick must be delivered with the same painstaking care that would go into an important putt in golf. As in golf, a fundamental rule applies on every kick—keep your eye on the ball."

Pressure never seemed to bother Manders. In 1933, his rookie season, the Bears faced the New York Giants in the league title match. Manders opened the scoring for the Bears with a 16-yard field goal, and he chipped in a second one from the

Jack Manders, the Bears' star kicker of the 1930's

40-yard line before the half ended. He booted a 28-yarder in the third period and, with two extra-point conversions, accounted for 11 of the Bears' 23 points in their 23–21 win. Manders and each of his teammates received $210.34 for their winning effort.

The next year was Manders' finest, as he led the league in scoring with 79 points. It was a banner year for the Bears, too. They roared through the 13-game season without a defeat. Once again they met the Giants for the league title, and once again the game was dominated by a kicker. But it wasn't Manders; it was Ken Strong of the Giants.

Strong had joined the New York club in 1933. He had been an outstanding college performer at New York University, leading the nation in scoring in 1928, his senior year. Then followed four years with the Staten Island Stapletons, an NFL team from 1929 to 1932.

Strong learned to kick field goals as a twelve-year-old in West Haven, Connecticut. There was no crossbar available for his practice sessions so he used a telephone wire, specializing in the drop kick. It wasn't until he arrived at NYU and came under the direction of coach Chick Meehan that he learned to place-kick.

Strong once kicked a field goal three times— the same field goal, that is. It happened in 1933, his first year with the Giants. He booted the field goal from the 15-yard line and the Giants were

Ken Strong, in a pose typical of the 1930's, was featured on the cover for the program of the 1934 NFL title game.

offside. He kicked it from the 20-yard line. Another offside. He made it from the 25-yard line, and this time it counted. The Giants won, beating the Bears, 3–0.

Strong was also one of the best punters of his time. He once described his punting style. "I'd stand flat-footed, and if the snap looked good I'd draw my left foot back a bit, then step out on my right, hop on my left, and kick. Just one-and-one-half steps. We didn't need a lot of steps because we punted from only nine or ten yards behind the center."

Despite his short approach, Strong was able to get enormous power into his punts. During the time he was a member of the Stapes, Strong once had a punt blocked by Bill Owens of the Giants, who hurtled over the line to stop the ball with his chest. The next day Owens happened to look in the mirror as he was getting dressed, and in the center of a large oval-shaped bruise on his chest he could make out the words: A.G. SPALDING CO. OFFICIAL LEAGUE FOOTBALL.

It was Strong who spearheaded the Giants to division championships in 1933 and 1934. He did not merely punt and place-kick. He blocked, ran, threw passes, and received them.

The championship game in 1934, played at New York's Polo Grounds with the Bears the opposition, was the legendary "sneakers game," in which the Giants switched to basketball shoes at half time so they could run and cut on the frozen field.

The Giants' only scoring in the first half came as a result of Strong's 38-yard field goal. The New Yorkers trailed, 10–3, when they came out onto the field in their fancy footwear for the third period. It started on a disasterous note for Strong. Attempting to kick off wearing sneakers, he lost the toenail from the big toe of his kicking foot. Fortunately, the injury didn't affect his running ability and he scored two touchdowns in the final quarter in New York's 30–13 victory. The game ranks as one of the biggest upsets in NFL history.

Strong stayed with the Giants through 1935, then switched to the New York Yanks of the rival American Football League after a salary dispute. There he stayed two years, returning to the Giants in 1939, the year that he retired—for the first time. When the New York team was hit with a wartime talent shortage in 1944, they asked Strong to return once more.

He agreed to, but only if he didn't have to run with the ball, just kick. Age had apparently ripened his talents, for he led the NFL in field goals that year with six. So confident was he that his teammates would protect him, that when he went into a game he wore no shoulder pads and seldom took off his wristwatch.

In 1947, when Strong retired for good, he held

Bob Waterfield of the Rams combined kicking with quarterbacking.

virtually all of the Giants' records for scoring and kicking. He was elected to membership in Pro Football's Hall of Fame in 1967.

Strong was the kicking coach for the Giants for many years after his retirement as a player. One of his protégés was Don Chandler. Ironically, Chandler became the player who broke many of Strong's records.

Chandler, like Strong, was both a place-kicker and punter. "If a fellow is a good straightaway punter," Strong says, "he should also be able to place-kick without it affecting his punting." He cites Bob Waterfield, Clarke Hinkle, and Dutch Clark as other successful two-way kickers. All, incidentally, are Hall of Fame members.

Now living on Long Island, a salesman, Strong can't understand why punters and place-kickers of the present day don't work harder to get more leg into the ball. "Any boy who has snap in his leg should be a good punter," he says. "Steps, balance, the proper drop, and follow-through—that's all it takes. And practice. I used to practice until my leg dropped off."

Players like Strong and Manders were unusual, however. The field goal was still held in low esteem. When a team got within 20 or 30 yards of the opposition end zone, the idea was to keep going for a touchdown. The Los Angeles Rams had a marvelous kicker in Bob Waterfield, who also happened to be the team's quarterback. Waterfield, in 1947, needed to boot only seven field goals to lead the league. In 1949 he was the league leader a second time—with nine.

Quarterbacks Sammy Baugh and Sid Luckman, and Don Hutson, an artist when it came to catching passes, were the players who dominated the game through the 1940's. Arnie Herber of the Green Bay Packers and Tommy Thompson were other noted players, and both won recognition by throwing the ball.

More change was coming, however. In April, 1942, with players being called into military service, club owners adopted the free-substitution rule, which permitted coaches to shuttle players on and off the field without restriction. Previously, when a substitution had been made, the player coming off the field could not return to the game in the same half.

Almost every player up to this time played "both ways," offense and defense. The ability to kick the ball, pass, or run with it was not enough. A man also had to have the strength, agility, and desire to play defense. But the unlimited substitution rule, which was made permanent by a unanimous vote of the owners in January, 1950, helped to change all that. It meant that a man could devote himself to the development of a particular skill, really work to perfect it. He remained on the sidelines until his specialty was needed, then entered the game rested and ready to perform.

Another change, an evolutionary one, that aided the cause of the kicker had to do with the size of team rosters. In 1949 rosters were limited to 32 players, so, despite the free-substitution rule, there were still not many real specialists. Players still had to be able to do something else besides whatever they did best. Gradually over the years the roster limit was raised—to 33 players in 1951, to 36 players in 1959, to 37 in 1964, and in 1967, a jump to 40 players, the limit today. With 40 players, a coach had enormous leeway. He could even have two kicking specialists—a place-kicker *and* a punter.

The kicking game—place-kicking at least—received another boost in January, 1948, when the plastic kicking tee won approval. But this was of minor importance compared to the impact exerted by the unlimited substitution rule combined with the bigger rosters.

The very first man to benefit from these various innovations and collect a paycheck for doing nothing more than kicking a football was a gypsy kicker named Ben Agajanian. Agajanian kicked for ten different teams, which in itself must be a record, in a career that spanned two decades. After a season or two with a team, he would retire but someone would always convince him to try again.

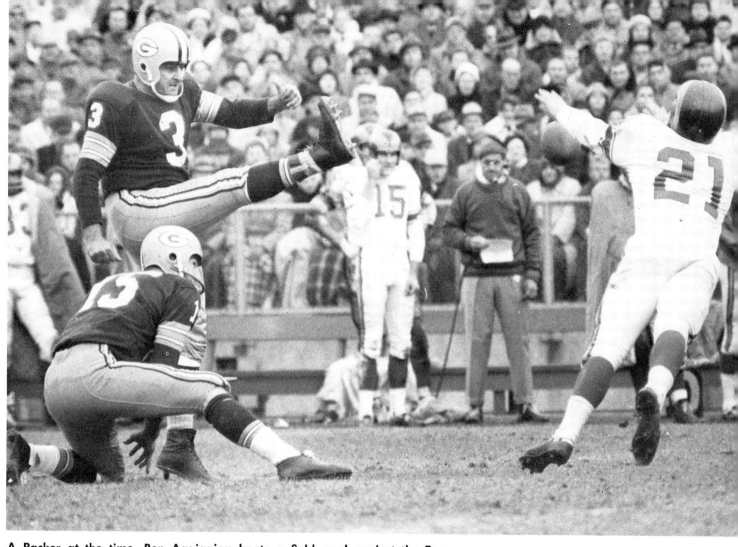

A Packer at the time, Ben Agajanian boots a field goal against the Rams.

Agajanian's career as a kicker had an unusual beginning. At Compton (California) Junior College, he reported to the football coach and was asked what position he played. "Tackle," said Agajanian. "So they put me at tackle for a while," he once recalled. "Then one day the coach pulled me aside and said, 'What else can you do?' I loved the game so I said, 'I kick, too.' I never kicked in my life but he told me to practice until he called me. I waited a long time but one day he did call."

In 1941, when Agajanian was twenty-two, he lost the toes of his kicking foot in a freight elevator accident. He was attending the University of New Mexico at the time, and a man in Albuquerque made him a special shoe to fit his toeless foot. It was wide and square across the top and looked much like one of today's kicking shoes, except that it was ankle high. Modern shoes are low cut.

After college and a tour of duty in the Army, which he managed to combine with three seasons of minor league football, Agajanian caught on with the Philadelphia Eagles as a tackle and also a kicker. This was 1945. "I was strong in the thighs and I weighed 190," he recalls. "I'd give those guys a hip and send them sprawling."

The same year the Eagles traded Agajanian to the Steelers. Not long after he arrived, Agajanian broke his arm and it was put in a cast. Although he couldn't play tackle, he still kicked. No one regarded his status as anything special, but in run-

Agajanian wore a special shoe to fit his toeless right foot.

ning on and off the field to boot field goals and extra points, his broken arm strapped to his chest, Agajanian was opening the era of the "pure" kicker.

Agajanian sat out 1946 and made his first comeback the following year with the Los Angeles Dons of the All America Football Conference. He led the league in field goals that season with 15, more than twice as many as the leader in the NFL. After a two-year stand with the Dons, Agajanian kicked

for the New York Giants (twice), the Los Angeles Rams, the Los Angeles Chargers, the Dallas Texans, the Green Bay Packers, and the Oakland Raiders.

He "quit for good" after a brief stay with Oakland, but two years later, at forty-five, he was back once more, this time with the San Diego Chargers. In his first game he behaved like a twenty-year old, kicking a 32-yard field goal, missing short on a 47-yarder, and making four extra points.

That *was* his last season. Agajanian played thirteen years in all, scoring 655 points, which placed him No. 15 on the all-time scoring list at the time of his retirement. He was, incidentally, the only player ever to perform in the AAFC, the AFL, and the NFL.

Agajanian, despite his talents, was never able to lead the NFL in field goals. The reason he wasn't was a big, broad-shouldered kicker with the Cleveland Browns by the name of Lou Groza. Groza's career pretty much paralleled that of Agajanian, stretching from 1946 to 1966, with a one-year hiatus in 1960. But in terms of achievement Groza was a great deal more successful. Indeed, he was the first player to win star status with his foot. "I don't think there can be any doubt," declared Browns' coach Paul Brown, "that Lou

An electric heater and wired socks help keep Agajanian's golden foot warm.

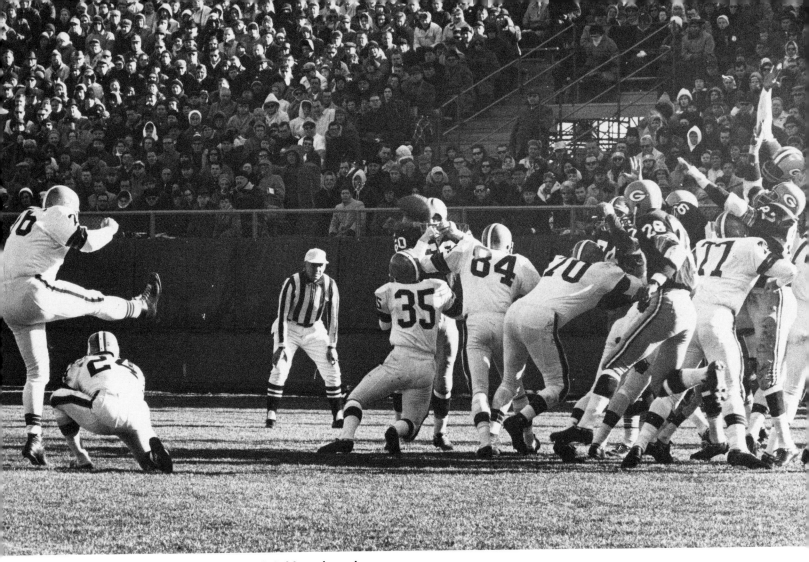

Lou Groza adds to his record field-goal total.

Groza is the finest place-kicker football has ever seen."

Statistics confirm Brown's opinion. Five times Groza led the NFL in field goals, a record no modern kicker has come close to equalling. In 1952 Groza booted a record 19 field goals; in 1953 he raised the total to 23.

The frequency with which Groza put the ball through the uprights helped to reestablish the field goal as a legitimate scoring weapon, not something a team merely "settled for." More than any other player, Lou Groza helped to lead the kicking game out of the dark ages.

Some of the credit must go to Paul Brown. After all, as coach of the Browns, it was he who gave Groza the opportunity to kick. Other coaches didn't use the field goal as often as Brown did, simply because they followed a conventional formula. Brown wouldn't; he broke the pattern.

Up until the final years of his career, Groza also played tackle. The concept of having the kicker do something else besides kick persisted well into the 1960's. Green Bay's Paul Hornung, a fine pressure kicker who played up until 1966, got paid almost entirely for the yards he gained as a running back. The Patriots' Gino Cappelletti, the best kicker of the old American League, was also a pass receiver. The practice finally ended during the 1970's, although there were occasional exceptions, the most noted being George Blanda of the Oakland Raiders, who not only kicked but served as the team's backup quarterback.

Recent years have also been significant for the outstanding success attained by soccer-style kickers. Players like Jan Stenerud, Garo Yepremian, and Horst Muhlmann have added a new dimension to the kicking game.

A recent change that worked to the benefit of kickers, one that became effective with the 1972 season, had to do with the playing field's in-bounds markers. Sometimes called hash marks, these are the guides that indicate to the officials where the ball is to be placed after a ball carrier goes out of bounds or is brought down close to the sideline.

The NFL rules committee, concerned about the decreasing number of touchdown passes in the seasons just prior to 1972, moved the in-bounds markers closer to the center of the field, slightly more than three yards closer. As it is now, the in-bounds markers are the same distance apart as the width of the goal post crossbar—18 feet, 6 inches. As this implies, the hash marks line up with the uprights.

The idea behind this was to give more operating room to the offense. But place-kickers were beneficiaries, too. No longer would they have to attempt kicks from sharp angles. Every kick became virtually straight on.

Because of the frequency with which kickers now boot extra points and field goals, they have

Soccer stylists like Jan Stenerud have given an added dimension to the modern kicking game.

attracted the attention of the men who make the rules. For example, to put excitement back into the conversion play after touchdown, it's been suggested that the 2-point option play be adopted. The kick for an extra point would still be worth one point, but a team that crossed the goal line from the 2-yard line by means of a pass or rush would earn two points.

College rules permit the 2-point option play and it was also used by the old American Football League. In the ten-year history of the AFL, a total of 3,190 touchdowns were scored. But coaches elected to try the 2-point play only 157 times, or about 5 per cent of the time. Eighty-five of the attempts were successful. When the two leagues merged, the 2-point option play was discarded.

Fans like the play because it adds to the suspense in a close game. In 1972, the *Sporting News* polled more than 1,300 fans and found that 92 per cent would like to see the 2-point play put into effect.

Others have suggested that a run or pass be made mandatory for the extra point, that the place kick be prohibited. Still others recommend that the extra-point play itself be done away with.

Suggestions for change are also frequently heard concerning the field goal. It is being said that the field goal was never meant to have the importance it has today. Some critics want to scale the value of a field goal according to the distance it is kicked.

For example, a field goal kicked inside the 20-yard line would be worth 2 points; one kicked from between the 20-30, 3 points; from the 30-40, 4 points; and so on. This isn't likely to happen because the rulesmakers don't like to tinker with point values. They feel they're disturbing the foundations of the game.

Another solution is simply to move the goal posts back to where they used to be, to the end line, which is ten yards behind the goal line. This is where the goal posts are in college football. What this would do is make a team advance the ball ten more yards than is now the case in order to get the same kind of field-goal chance. The proposal would also make less certain the try for point after touchdown.

Such rule changes aren't going to be instituted right away. But even if they were, it's not likely they would serve to diminish the importance of the kicking game to any significant degree. Today's kickers, toe-kickers and soccer stylists alike, have advanced their art to such an extent that it will take much more than a mere rule change to lessen their eminence.

The trend is clear: in the years to come there will be more kicks and longer kicks, and kickers are likely to become even more accurate than they are now. The foot is back in football to stay.

Pete Gogolak, first of the soccer stylists

THE FINE ART OF PLACE-KICKING

Putting a 15-ounce football over a horizontal bar that is set 10 feet above the ground and through the 18½-foot zone that separates the goal posts, and doing it with your foot, is no easy task. It takes superb coordination, the ability to swing one's foot into the ball with such perfect timing that the momentum of the approach—that energy—is transferred to the point of contact.

The drop kick used to be the more accepted method of accomplishing this but now the place kick is pre-eminent. For years, football experts thought they knew all there was to know about the place kick. It was simple: the man who was to kick stood several feet directly behind the ball, concentrated on the spot where it was to be placed, then started forward, striding first with his right foot, then his left, then kicking, the hard toe of the kicking shoe punching the ball up and away.

Then along came Pete Gogolak. Born in Budapest, Pete, his two brothers, and their parents fled Hungary in 1956 following the revolt and Russian take-over, and settled in upstate New York. As a high school sophomore, Pete was disappointed to find the school had no soccer team, because he had played on a junior championship team in Budapest. A classmate suggested he might enjoy football. When the coach asked for kickers, Pete tried out.

Wearing soft soccer shoes, Pete approached the ball obliquely instead of straight on, planted his left foot, then slapped the ball with the side of his right foot. His strong soccer-developed legs enabled him to whack long, low, line drives. The coach let him kick off that year, but that was all. The following summer Pete worked with his brother Charlie to improve what he was now calling the "Gogolak method," and the next season he did all of the team's kicking. College talent scouts were impressed with his skill and out of the several scholarship offers he received, Pete chose Cornell.

He didn't get a chance to try many field goals there, but he kicked 54 of 55 extra points, including 44 in a row, a collegiate record at the time. But pro football scouts had their doubts. After all, who ever heard of kicking a football with the instep.

Harvey Johnson, Director of Player Personnel for the Buffalo Bills, was less skeptical than his colleagues. One fall afternoon in 1963 he drove over to the Cornell campus at Ithaca to watch Gogolak work out. Pete kicked some short ones, then started backing up, to the 40, the 45, the 50. "Now want to see me kick some long ones?" Pete asked.

Johnson shook his head. "I was afraid he'd pull a muscle," he said afterward. "Besides, I figured he was going to cost us enough as it was."

As a rookie with the Bills, Pete kicked 45 out of 46 extra points, 19 of 28 field goals, and scored eight of the Bills' 20 points in their win over San Diego in the AFL title game. The following season, as if to prove his rookie year was no fluke, Gogolak set an AFL record for field goals with 28. He left the Bills in 1966 to sign with the New York Giants.

Pete Gogolak opened a new era for the kicking game. After he demonstrated what could be done with the instep, the rush to find soccer-style kickers was on.

Pro football's tackles, guards, running backs, quarterbacks, and all other players are channeled into the game by means of the NFL's annual selection meeting—the draft. In the draft, teams select the players with whom they wish to negotiate from the pool of graduating college seniors.

Why doesn't this hold true for place-kickers? Why go to Europe in search of soccer stylists?

One reason is because there is not enough emphasis on teaching the kicking game in high schools and colleges. Few coaches are qualified to teach it; others simply don't have the time.

Another reason is that the college kicking game is different from the pro version. The goal posts are ten yards behind the goal line, whereas in pro ball they're right on the goal. The in-bounds markers are 15 feet closer to the sidelines. The tee that college kickers use when kicking off is higher. No one can tell how all of these factors are going to affect what seems to be a promising young kicker.

A European talent search by Hank Stram uncovered Jets' Bobby Howfield (left) and Bengal's Horst Muhlmann.

It's risky to give up a high draft choice for one.

By the late 1960's, soccer-style place-kickers were fully accepted in pro football. Each summer, scouts combed Europe in search of talent. A look at rosters of 1972 is evidence of their success: the Jets' kicker was from England; the Chiefs' from Norway; in Dallas, an Austrian did the kicking; in Cincinnati, a German. The Miami Dolphins had an Armenian place-kicker who came to the United States by way of Cyprus. The New England Patriots had a Hungarian—Pete Gogolak's kid brother, Charlie.

Hank Stram, coach of the Kansas City Chiefs, once led a European talent search that turned up not one star but two of them—Horst Muhlmann from West Germany, who was traded to the Cincinnati Bengals in 1969, and Bobby Howfield from England, who went to Denver in 1968 and then to the New York Jets. Howfield took part in Stram's clinic because a friend of his bet him a pint of beer that he wouldn't be successful. He amazed Stram by kicking off 68 yards with his right foot, then 62 yards with his left foot.

The most unusual talent hunt in recent years involved the New England Patriots. Conducted during the summer of 1971, it became known as "The Search for Superfoot." It began when a trio of Boston sports broadcasters began chiding the Patriots for their lack of kicking talent, and took it upon themselves to enlist the support of BOAC, the British national airline, and the London *Daily Mirror* to overcome the failing.

The *Daily Mirror*, the paper with the largest circulation in the Western world, was particularly enthusiastic. "Superfoot is wanted by an American-style football team," the paper declared, then went on to explain the game and the kicker's role. "The players turn out like spacemen in helmets and pounds of padding . . . they wear headguards with built-in facemasks, and padding for shoulders, ribs, forearms, knuckles, hips, thighs, and knees.

"But not Superfoot. He sits on the touchline until he is called on to kick goals." Headlines in the paper proclaimed: "Who is Superfoot?" "Where is he?"

Almost 700 contestants, amateur soccer and rugby players, entered the competition. First prize was $1,000 and a contract with the Patriots. Coach John Mazur and personnel director Bucko Kilroy went to London to make the final decision.

The kickers who had qualified were brought to an American air base near London for the final competition. An American football team scrimmaged for the contestants so they could get an idea of what the game was like. They stared open-mouthed at the football uniforms. "They look like bloody moon-walkers," said one of them.

The winner was a genial twenty-one-year-old bricklayer from Lancaster named Mike Walker. He boomed two 55-yard field goals in the finals and at least half a dozen others of more than 50 yards distance.

In the United States that fall, Walker lost out to Charlie Gogolak in competition for a job with the Patriots. But being a determined young man, Walker went home and practiced and came back the next year to try again. His first appearance

Patriots' Mike Walker warms up his super foot.

before home fans came in a preseason game against the Chicago Bears. He booted two field goals and missed three, one a 63-yarder.

"I was tense," he said afterward. "It was the first time I played before hometown fans. But I can make a 63-yard kick. I know I can."

Actually, there is very little in the game of soccer that involves kicking the ball the way a placekicker kicks it. A soccer player uses his instep to advance the ball, to dribble it, but seldom is there an opportunity to take two or three well-timed steps before kicking. The soccer ball is always moving, or almost always.

What makes soccer valuable is that the sport is ideal for conditioning the legs. Only basketball among the popular American sports is anywhere its equal in this regard. And strong legs make for long kicks.

Garo Yepremian of the Miami Dolphins, one of the most successful kickers of recent years, doesn't believe that the sidewinding style he uses gives him any advantage over American straight-on kickers. But European kickers have an edge, says Yepremian, because they begin earlier. "They develop strong legs because they start kicking the ball when they're four or five," he states. "Americans begin kicking later—after they've tried out for the team at another position and decided that they're going to have trouble making it.

"Kids are always asking, 'Should I change my

Horst Muhlmann, a leading practitioner . . .

style?' I tell them no, just kick the way you're used to kicking. Kids who are used to straight-toe kicking can be just as successful as us, if they keep on with it."

Kicking becomes instinctive to a boy who is

. . . **demonstrates the soccer style of place-kicking.**

trained for soccer. In many parts of Europe, when a youngster goes to school in the morning he dribbles a soccer ball on the way. American sports are hand oriented. Throw a ball to an American youngster and he'll put up his hands to catch it.

Not a European boy; he'll block with his chest or shoulder, let it drop to the ground, then kick it back.

This instinct has manifested itself on the football field. Pete Gogolak once tried a field goal

Austria's Toni Fritsch handles Cowboys' kicking chores.

against the Cowboys and one of the Dallas players catapulted over the line to block the ball with his chest. It rebounded toward Gogolak whose reflexes took command. Instead of trying to recover the ball, he kicked it with his left foot and it went right through the uprights.

No one on the field had ever seen a play like that, including the officials. But they ruled quickly. In the first place, kicking a loose ball is illegal. In the second place, because the ball went beyond the Dallas goal, a touchback was ruled. The Cowboys, after refusing to accept a penalty (which would have given the Giants another chance at the field goal) took possession on the 20-yard line.

Of the two kicking styles, the American toe-method is the least complicated. It involves a three-step approach—a short, unhurried step with the kicking foot, the right foot, then a "power step" with the left, then the kick. (Sometimes this is called a two-step approach; other times a two-and-one-half step approach.)

The left foot, sometimes called the "plant" foot, is placed down—"planted"—two or three inches to the left of the ball and six or seven inches in back of it. As the kicking leg comes forward, the knee is flexed, but it locks, comes rigid, as the toe makes contact.

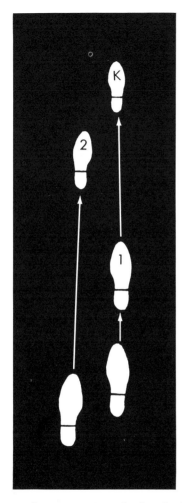

Toe-kickers employ an approach that looks like this, kicking on the final step.

Most kickers line up with the goal posts and then stare at the spot where the ball is to be placed, and that's all they look at until the leg swings through. They aim about two or three inches below the middle of the ball. But a kicker's target may vary. When attempting an extra point, and thus trying to get the ball up quickly, he may target lower on the ball than is normal. On a long field-goal attempt, where a low trajectory is required, he is likely to hit more toward the ball's middle.

Most kickers will tell you that they use essentially the same technique on field goals as they do on extra points. Varying one's approach or the kick itself causes difficulties. For instance, on a very long field-goal attempt, one of 45 yards or more, there's a tendency for the kicker to speed his approach and overpower the ball. When this happens the ball may fall short of the goal line by 10 or 15 yards. The kicker has to be natural—every time.

Most place-kickers follow through, although some of the soccer-style booters don't. But every kicker, no matter what his style, strives to keep his head down as his right foot swings through. Otherwise, his foot won't hit the target.

The temptation to look up is difficult to resist. During the 1967 season, Jim Bakken of the St. Louis Cardinals broke the record of six field goals in a game by kicking seven. He almost had eight. In the game's closing minutes, Bakken missed an

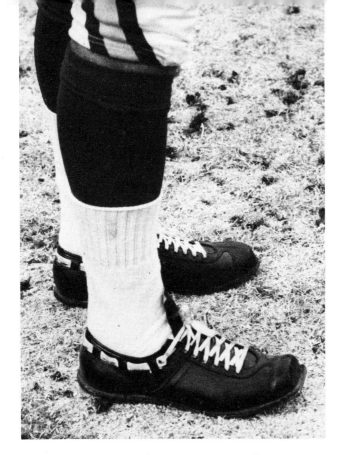

Fred Cox's kicking shoe has conventional square toe.

easy 23-yarder. "I was too excited. I wanted to see badly if it was good," he recalls, "and I looked up too quickly." His foot failed to hit the ball squarely; the kick went wide.

In the case of toe-kickers, the right shoe, the one that does the kicking, is of special construction. The hard toe is box-shaped; it thus strikes the ball squarely, and even allows for a slight margin of error. The sole is reinforced with a thin metal plate. The other shoe, the left shoe, is of conventional design.

League rules permit only shoes that are standard production models. "It has to be the same type of shoe that any high school youngster can pick up in a sporting goods store," says an NFL official. "And the shoe can't be doctored in any way."

In days past, some kickers used extra-long laces, which they would tie in back of the ankle. This caused the front of the shoe to tilt upward at an angle that was perfect for place-kicking. Such tactics aren't allowed nowadays.

Soccer-style kickers don't require square-toed shoes. All they want is a soft, comfortable shoe, like a soccer shoe but with cleats.

The soccer-style kicker doesn't stand directly in back of the ball the way the toe-kicker does. He lines up at about a 45-degree angle with the ball. And with many, the first step is with the balance foot, not the kicking foot. It's left step, right stride, left stride, right kick.

And whereas the toe-kicker simply steps forward to hammer the ball toward the target, the soccer stylist balances for a split second on his left foot, then sweeps his right foot into the ball.

It is generally agreed that the soccer-type kicker,

The blocking looks like this on extra-point and field-goal tries.

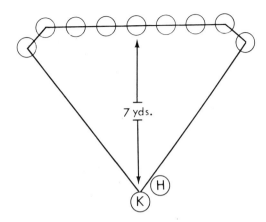

On field-goal and extra-point attempts, blockers set up a cone of protection for the kicker.

since he's able to take a wider swing with his leg, gets more power into the kick, and power means distance. But every kicker will tell you that power is not the most important thing, that accuracy is what really counts, and in this regard the toe-kicker has the advantage. Since he uses a straight-line approach, he's able to aim with greater precision. And he's also able to follow through more naturally, more efficiently, which helps him to be accurate.

To protect the kicker on field-goal tries and extra-point attempts, the kicking team employs a tight, balanced line, with the interior linemen protecting to the inside. A blocker is also stationed behind and just outside each end. Each has the

responsibility of delaying the rushmen who take the outside route.

The kicker must get the kick away in about 1.4 seconds. "You're rushing if you kick in less than 1.3 seconds," says the Chiefs' Jan Stenerud. "But if you don't get the ball away in less than 1.5 seconds, you get it back in your face."

One might think that if the ball was spotted farther back, say nine yards behind the line of scrimmage, the kicker would have more time, but

To check Pete Gogolak's kicking efficiency, Giant Coach Jim Garrett consults a stopwatch.

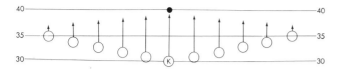

Some teams line up like this on kickoffs . . .

it doesn't work that way. When the ball is spotted deeper, the defending players at opposite sides of the line of scrimmage have a direct path to the kicker. But when the ball is placed down at seven yards, they have to hook around the kicking team's blockers, and this delays them.

The place kick used in kicking off is different from the one used in field-goal or extra-point attempts in that there is a longer approach. Some kickers take as much as a ten-yard run at the ball. The first few steps are short and unhurried. Gradually they increase in length and speed until, at impact, the kicker is really moving, and he's thus able to get the full force of his body into the kick.

Another difference with the kickoff is that the ball can be teed-up on a plastic kicking tee. Since the ball is slightly elevated, the kicker can feel confident that the cleats of his kicking foot aren't

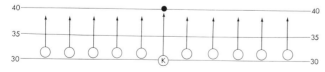

. . . others, like this.

Fred Cox, kicking off, launches his body into the ball.

going to scuff the ground, or that the holder isn't going to get him down in some fashion, as occasionally happens on field-goal tries. Overall, it's a surer, cleaner kick.

The idea on the kickoff is to drive the ball beyond the end zone. Then it can't be run back. Just as good is the kick that strikes one of the goal posts or the crossbar. The rules don't permit these to be run back either.

Coaches have no complaint when the ball is kicked with good height several yards deep into the end zone, because then the return man has to decide whether to run the ball out. If he decides not to, putting one knee to the turf after making the catch—an act one sportswriter has branded as the "chicken kneel"—his team gets the ball on its 20-yard line. If he does try to run it out, it's not likely he will get very far, probably to the 20 or 25-yard line.

A kick that has good height but comes down around the 10-yard line isn't looked upon with favor. There's too great a chance for a long runback. The worst type of kick is the one that is both low and short.

In achieving good distance on kickoffs, the most important element is to be consistent. The kicker has to use the same number of steps and the same approach speed on every kick. If his approach is particularly fast, and he happens to hit the ball just right, he may blast it for an all-time record. But if

he fails to get a perfect hit, the ball may veer to the left or right. So instead of approaching at full speed, kickers tend to be deliberate. They want the ball to boom away but they also want to be

Charlie Gogolak (7) is evidence that great size isn't necessary to be a place-kicker.

accurate, and the latter is more important than the former.

Another key factor is the left foot and where it is placed down. If it's planted too close to the ball, the right foot, when it swings through, is likely to strike too low on the ball and a short kick results. If the left foot is placed down too great a distance from the ball, the right foot may hit in the center of the ball or even above the center, and the result is a kick that travels low and not very far. Every kicker works on getting and maintaining proper placement of the left foot.

One's size is almost no factor in place-kicking. Garo Yepremian of the Dolphins stands 5-foot-7 and weighs 170. Charlie Gogolak of the Patriots is a couple of inches taller. Height doesn't hurt, however. The Chiefs' Jan Stenerud is a lanky 6-foot-2, 190.

It's interesting to note, however, that the newer toe-kickers are big men who can get good power. There's Curt Knight of the Redskins (6-foot-2, 190), David Ray of the Rams (6-foot, 195), and Jim O'Brien of the Colts (6-foot, 200).

Virtually all kickers are right-footed. But, again, it doesn't make any difference. Being left-footed certainly hasn't hindered the career of the Dolphins' Garo Yepremian. But whether your kicking leg is your left one or your right, it has to be strong, with particular development in the muscle area just above the knee.

The weather is an important factor in place-kicking. There's the wind, for instance. The first thing a kicker does when he goes out onto the field before a game is to check the wind, trying to

Curt Knight of the Redskins is one of the game's most reliable toe-kickers.

get some idea of its direction and velocity. He checks stadium flags or distant smokestacks, or he may toss a few blades of grass into the air (if the game isn't being played on artificial turf).

Sometimes it's difficult to judge how the wind is behaving. At circular Shea Stadium in New York, which is right on Flushing Bay, the wind whips in the same end that it goes out, and it swirls around so erratically that it seems to be coming from several directions at once. There are also strong and tricky winds at Candlestick Park in San Francisco, and at Cleveland Stadium, which is on Lake Erie.

A following wind is not the blessing that most people believe. It can cause the ball to drift right or left. Crosswinds are even a greater problem, of course. If the wind is blowing from left to right, say, and it's particularly strong, the kicker may try to compensate by adjusting his target to the left, but most prefer simply to aim at the middle of the goal posts and hit hard. They don't like to tinker.

Rain is a problem because it means the turf gets soggy. A kicker has to be able to plant his left foot solidly. If the foot slips, or even if he starts thinking he might slip, he can miss.

The kicker gets the credit when the kick is good and has to shoulder the blame when it goes awry. But it's not all his doing. Successful kicking is the result of teamwork, a smooth and coordinated effort on the part of the center, the holder, and kicker. When a kick is good, it's because each man

has done his job well. A bad kick results when one of the trio fails to perform his job in proper fashion.

Pete Gogolak once said that kicking field goals was 50 per cent physical ability, 30 per cent mental stability, while the remaining 20 per cent was the holder. "If the ball isn't set up right, you don't make it," says Gogolak, "no matter how good you are.

"If I see the laces I get nervous. They give you a bad kicking surface. The ball can go either way."

In quarterback Gary Wood, Gogolak had the same holder for years. Wood held for Gogolak in college, at Cornell, and the two teamed up again in 1966 after Pete signed with the New York Giants. When the Giants dropped Wood in 1969, Pete had to find a new holder. He decided on Fran Tarkenton, the team's quarterback at the time. "He had the quickest hands on the team," Gogolak explained. When Tarkenton was traded in 1972, Gogolak picked out punter Tom Blanchard to do his holding.

Most holders kneel on their right knee, bend their left leg, and place their left foot, which is lined up with the ball, flat to the ground. From this position the man can reach easily in any direction to grab a snap that may be off the mark.

Once the holder's hands are positioned for the catch, they act as a target for the center. The holder must make the catch, place it on the spot, spin the laces away from the kicker with his right

The ball is gone but the finger remains, evidence of a good hold by New York's Tom Blanchard.

hand, and hold the ball there with his left index finger—and he has to do all this in one second flat. The kicker then boots the ball out from under the finger.

The holder and the kicker agree beforehand where the ball will be placed down. If the holder happens to be the team's quarterback, he usually knows much more about the condition of the playing field than anyone else, and the kicker follows his advice as to where to place the ball. In Super Bowl IV, after the Chiefs had scored a second-period touchdown against the Vikings, Jan Stenerud came out onto the field for the extra-point attempt. Quarterback Len Dawson, Stenerud's holder, knew that the ground was soft and spongy at the spot where the ball was to be placed. He asked the referee to move the line of scrimmage back two yards, where the ground was solid. (A team can decide where it wants the line of scrimmage on extra-point attempts, but the ball cannot be spotted inside the two-yard line.)

The referee stepped off the two yards. Dawson held. Stenerud kicked. *Perfect.*

Sure hands are a "must" requirement for the holder. It's no accident that a team's holder is often its No. 1 quarterback, the man with the surest hands on the squad. Quarterback Len Dawson does the ball-holding for the Chiefs, John Brodie for the 49ers, and Sonny Jurgensen for the Redskins.

It's also good to have a passer as holder because he occasionally may be forced to throw the ball. Bobby Douglass, the Chicago Bears' quarterback who holds on placements, recovered an elusive snap during a game in 1971, retreated to the 35-yard line, and then threw a desperation pass to linebacker Dick Butkus in the end zone. Butkus was an eligible receiver because he was a backfield blocker on the play. The one point the play netted

was the Bears' margin of victory. Quarterback Bob Davis of the Jets passed to linebacker Ralph Baker under similar circumstances the same year.

Except for occasional feats of glory like these, the holder is seldom noticed. And usually when he does get his name in the paper he's not happy about it. During 1972 preseason play, Karl Noonan, holder for the Miami Dolphins, chased an errant snap that went over his head. At just about the same time that Noonan caught up with the ball, a horde of enemy players caught up with Noonan and trampled him to the ground. The next day Noonan's name was in the headlines from coast to coast. He had suffered a shoulder separation.

The center's job is punishing, too. When he looks back through his legs at the holder, he's vulnerable to attack from the opposition tackles. "They can really tee off on you," says center Mick Tingelhoff of the Vikings. "And sometimes they do." This doesn't happen when the center snaps the ball back to the quarterback. Then his head is up, and at the same time he's handing the ball back he's launching a block of his own.

Center Jim Otto of the Oakland Raiders, whose career began in 1960 and extended for well over a decade, bore the evidence of the punishment that men who play the position must absorb. His nose

"Grizzled veteran" is the way center Jim Otto was often described.

was broken so many times that the bridge was permanently flattened, and his lips cut so often that he had a crooked smile. Toward the end of his career he had to cover the back of his neck with sponge-rubber protection to reduce the chance of having nerves pinched again, and his helmet was equipped with a special lining to minimize the chances of another concussion. Of course, not every injury that Otto sustained came while centering on kicking plays, but many of the more serious ones did.

Even though the center knows that he's going to get hit and hit hard, he can't let it distract him. He's got to concentrate on getting the ball back.

There's a knack to centering. The first thing the center has to do is get properly balanced, his legs well spread and his weight evenly distributed on the balls of his feet. He takes his stance about an arm's length from the football and is careful to note· whether the laces are positioned correctly. Some centers like the laces straight down; others want them facing to the left. The laces are used to get a firm grip.

Whether the center is passing back to a holder or to a punter, he must spiral the ball back, so he grips it as if he were going to throw a forward pass. The right hand and arm supply the power of the snap; the left hand merely guides.

He has to slide his hand in place; the rules say that you can't pick up the ball. To assure the pass

Jets' Paul Crane grips the ball about like a quarterback does to pass it back.

is a crisp one, he snaps his wrist as he releases. He lets the ball roll off his fingertips; this helps to make it spiral. He also follows through.

The center uses the holder's hands as his target.

If he's really skilled, he snaps the ball so that it arrives with the laces straight up, which means that the holder doesn't have to waste time turning the ball. The center knows the holder is going to be seven yards away. He knows how many times the ball will revolve over that distance. (Usually it's one-and-one-half revolutions.) The rest is practice.

Coaches time the center just as carefully as they do the kicker. On a field-goal try, the center is given one-half a second to get the ball to the holder. On a punt he has more time—.7 of a second.

Sometimes a kicker, holder, and center will remain together for years, developing into a finely tuned unit. Then when one of the trio departs, either through retirement or injury, the machine-like performance of the other members of the unit suffers.

But not always. On September 24, 1967, when Jim Bakken of the St. Louis Cardinals set an all-time single-game record for field goals with seven, he had both a substitute holder and center. Larry Wilson, the Cards' regular holder, injured a hand and had to leave the game. Bobby Joe Conrad, a wide receiver, replaced him. Irv Goode had to take over for starting center Bob DeMarco when he was injured. With Conrad holding and Goode centering, Bakken kicked three field goals in the final

quarter. The last field goal, the record-breaker, was a 23-yarder.

"In practically every kicking situation, the center and holder are as important as the kicker," Bakken said afterward. "There's a delicate timing involved which isn't possible unless the same people work together in practice all the time. But today we were lucky."

There's one other aspect of place-kicking that must be mentioned. It's the psychological aspect of the job. Whether you kick with your toe or instep, you're bound to feel the emotional stress.

Part of the problem is that kickers spend 99 per cent of their time standing around waiting to kick. Even in a free-scoring game, one that involves several field-goal and extra-point attempts, a kicker's playing time is not likely to total a full minute. The rest of the time he spends watching from the sidelines, trying to keep involved. He has to keep himself fired up. Listless kickers end up doing public relations work for sporting goods companies.

Many kickers are pacers and walk several nervous miles during a game. Others stand and watch the game carefully, yelling encouragement to their teammates. Still others sit and fidget. Tom Dempsey spends time hurling insults at the game officials.

The pressure is increased by the fact that the kicker isn't supposed to miss. Perfection is the norm.

"A kicker wears only one hat," Jim Turner of the Denver Broncos once remarked. "You either make it or you miss. You're either a hero or a goat. And there's never a second chance."

Fred Cox paces the sidelines at Yankee Stadium.

SOME OF THE BEST

Out onto the field trots a good-sized man with a thickset body, his fists clenched, his shoulders set confidently. He wears a jet black jersey with a white 16. There is a dour face below the crinkled brow and bushy gray sideburns poke from beneath the silver helmet.

After a whispered conference with the man who will hold, he positions himself, his arms at his side, his eyes fixed to the spot where the ball is to be placed.

As the holder reaches for the ball, he starts forward, a short step with his right foot, a longer stride with his left, and then the right foot whips through, thumping the ball upward above the up-stretched arms and over the crossbar. He hardly notices the official's hands go up.

Ol' George Blanda has done it again. With every PAT or field goal he kicked, he set a scoring record.

Ol' George Blanda did it for twenty years and then some. He scored in more consecutive games than anyone else. He led the league in extra points more times. He threw more passes in a single game than anyone and completed more. He threw more touchdown passes in a single season—36—than anybody else (a record he shares with Y.A. Tittle), and he once threw seven touchdown passes in a game (a record he shares with several players).

With one second left in the final quarter, Blanda boots the winning point against the Jets.

A specialty of Blanda was to come in off the bench and kick a winning field goal or throw a winning pass. If the NFL record manual had a category, "Miracle Finishes, Career," Ol' George's name would be No. 1.

Blanda could come into a game in a critical situation, with the crowd screaming, and not show a trace of emotion. "Why not?" he once said. "I've made winning field goals in the last seconds; I've missed them. I've thrown touchdown passes that won games; I've thrown interceptions that lost them. What else can happen to me?"

Blanda dominates pro football's longevity records, too, playing in more seasons and more games than anyone. When Blanda played his first season, Daryle Lamonica, the future quarterback for the Oakland Raiders and the man to hold for George's place kicks, was in third grade. Some of his 1970 teammates weren't even born.

"I've been lucky," Blanda once said. "I've only been hurt once. That's why I've been able to last so long."

A diligent year-round exercise program also helped. During the off-season, Blanda played handball several times a week and also golfed. As the season drew near, he would begin running several miles a day. He wouldn't do any throwing or kicking until he arrived at training camp. Then he'd start out slowly, gradually bringing his arm and leg into tune. The coaches left him alone,

allowing him to set his own pace.

"I'm in better shape now than I was a few years ago," he said not long after his forty-fourth birthday. "The most important thing is whether you love the game, and I still do. Playing football is damn good fun."

George Frederick Blanda was born on September 17, 1927, the year that Lindbergh flew the Atlantic Ocean and Babe Ruth hit all those home runs. The place was Youngwood, Pennsylvania, eighteen miles southeast of Pittsburgh, in the heart of the coal country. His parents were Slovak immigrants and his father worked in the mines. There were six brothers and four sisters. "We competed for everything," Blanda once said, "even for the food on the table."

As a boy growing up, one of the things Blanda wanted most was a bus ticket out of town. He earned it through football, winning a scholarship to the University of Kentucky. As a quarterback for Coach Bear Bryant, he guided Kentucky to a couple of bowl games, and when he graduated in 1949 the Chicago Bears signed him.

Pro football was much different then. There was a team in New York called the Bulldogs, and the Cardinals were based in Chicago. Baltimore and San Francisco hadn't come into the league yet. It was a time well before packed stadiums were to become commonplace, a time before national television coverage of games. When Blanda signed, he received $600, not as a bonus but as an advance against his salary. It was a loan, actually.

Being with Chicago was not a happy experience for Blanda. Mention the Bears to him today and his face turns sour. He started out as Chicago's No. 3 quarterback and he also did some linebacking. About the only real contribution he made was as a field-goal kicker. As a rookie, he booted seven; the league high that year was nine. In his third season with the Bears, Blanda also became the team's specialist on extra-point attempts, and in 1957 he led the league with 45.

Despite these achievements, Blanda preferred quarterbacking to kicking. But George Halas, owner of the Bears and the team's coach at the time, never really regarded Blanda as being a skilled signal caller, and used him as the Bears' full-time quarterback only once, in 1953. The other years Blanda warmed the bench, waiting for someone to get injured or traded. Halas never squandered any money on Blanda either. When George needed a toe for his kicking shoe, he had to buy his own.

After ten years of neglect and low wages, Blanda quit the Bears. He quit pro football, in fact, and went to work as a salesman for a trucking company. When the American Football League set up operations in 1960, the club owners went looking for experienced quarterbacks. Blanda became a Houston Oiler—at thirty-three.

No quarterback before or since ever passed the football with the frequency and effect that Blanda did in Houston. Many an afternoon he darkened the Texas sky with footballs. In a game in 1961, he gained 464 yards passing, and in 1964 he attempted a record 505 passes for the season, and in one game he threw 68 of them, completing a record 37. In pro football, to *throw* 37 passes in a game is an accomplishment. Three times Blanda led the Oilers to a division title and twice to the league championship.

Blanda seldom went for the bomb, the long touchdown throw. He threw a flat, fast pass that never got far above the ground. He was a control passer.

Then in the mid-1960's, his control began to desert him. He led the league in interceptions several times and began to hear sharp criticism. Despite a couple of horrible preseason games in 1966, Blanda was again named the Oilers' No. 1 quarterback for the season ahead. Jack Gallagher of the Houston *Post*, who sometimes called Blanda "Old Hippety Hop," commented that it was a "case of turning disorder into catastrophe." Said Gallagher, "Had the 1876 Congress operated in a similar fashion, a Medal of Honor might have been struck for George Custer."

As quarterback for the Houston Oilers, Blanda set countless AFL passing records.

"Every defensive back in the AFL roots for Blanda's return," said another writer. The fans had mixed feelings. Signs hung in the stadium expressed their sentiments. "Blanda Must Go!" was a popular one. But some were affectionate, like "George, You're the Greatest."

The people who supported Blanda were probably won over by his kicking. His arm might have been erratic but his foot was sublime. In the American League record manual, under the heading "Most Points After Touchdown, Season," Blanda, with 64, is No. 1. He is also No. 2 and No. 3. Five times he led the league in PATs, and he probably would have been a frequent leader in field goals, too, if anyone but Gino Cappelletti (see below) had been the competition. But as it is, Blanda holds the AFL record for the longest field goal, a 55-yarder against San Diego in 1961.

In the end the critics won out. Blanda was put on waivers in 1967, which meant that Houston was no longer interested in his services, that any other club could have him for a pittance, namely the $100 waiver fee. Oakland picked him up. In his seven seasons with the Oilers, George established nineteen career, season, and game records. Of course, the records were worth absolutely nothing at the Oakland training camp that fall, and Blanda, at thirty-nine, had to demonstrate for the

Blanda treats his foot to a blast of heated air.

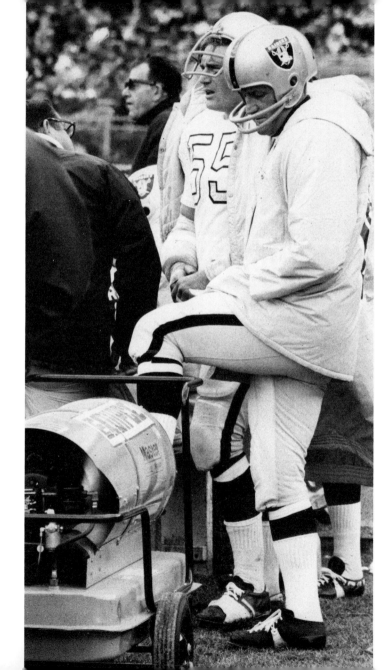

umpteenth time that he wasn't washed up.

"My foot has kept me in this game," Blanda has said many times. It surely applied to this phase of his career. The Raiders were rich in quarterbacks, with the splendid Daryle Lamonica heading the list. George started out as the No. 4 man but by the time the season opened he was playing right behind Lamonica.

Over the next three years, Blanda caused no great excitement. As the Raiders place-kicking specialist, he was more than adequate. He led the league in PATs with 56 in his first year with the team, and again in 1969 with 45. He was consistently among the leaders in field goals. And any time Lamonica got hurt, George would be rushed in. He began to develop a reputation as a fine clutch passer.

Blanda had no illusions, however, A few days before the 1970 season opened, and, as it happened, a few days before his forty-third birthday, the Raiders put Blanda on waivers. "My age is against me," he told columnist Larry Merchant. "A team has to look for younger players."

That could easily have been the end. He already had twenty seasons as an active player, which was three more seasons than any other player ever had. He was prepared to go back home to his wife and daughter in LaGrange, Illinois, and to his job as a trucking company executive. But when no one entered a claim, the Raiders decided to keep him.

It has to be ranked as the outstanding decision of the season.

A game in Pittsburgh late in October began a string of five incredible weeks in a row. After Lamonica was injured, Blanda came in late in the first period. With the score tied, 7–7, and in the face of a ferocious blitz, he passed 44 yards for another touchdown. That was in the first half. In the second half, he passed for another touchdown and the Raiders won, 31–14.

The next week Kansas City was George's victim. On the next to last play of the game, Blanda kicked a 48-yard field goal to get the Raiders a 17–17 tie.

The following week was even more dramatic. The Raiders trailed the Browns, 17–13, with eleven minutes remaining when Lamonica was injured. A Cleveland field goal made it 20–13, but then Ol' George went to work. He connected with Warren Wells for a 14-yard touchdown, then kicked the extra point to tie the score.

Less than two minutes were left and the Browns had possession. An interception set the stage for Blanda to try a field goal from the Raiders' 48. With three seconds remaining, he pounded the ball over the bar to win the game.

Miracle No. 4 came against the Broncos. After Lamonica had reinjured his shoulder, Blanda came in with four minutes left and the Raiders behind, to fire the winning touchdown pass. He also contributed a field goal and three extra points.

George Blanda has a word for the Jets' John Elliot.

"Pride and Poise" is the motto of the Raiders. After what Blanda did the fifth week, someone suggested changing the motto to "Pride, Poise, and George Blanda." He kicked a field goal with seven seconds left, to give the Raiders a 20–17 win over San Diego.

In Detroit on Thanksgiving Day, Blanda's miracle string ended. Replacing Lamonica in the fourth quarter, with the Raiders seven points behind, he completed five of eight passes, the last a 37-yarder to Ray Chester that brought Oakland to the Detroit 3-yard line, but the Raiders were offside and the play was nullified. George got no more chances that day.

He did get his magic working again in New York against the Jets the following week. With only seconds left, Lamonica unloaded a desperation pass to Warren Wells in the Jets' end zone that boosted the Raiders into a tie. With one second on the clock, Blanda kicked the game-winning point.

When the season ended, Blanda found himself the sensation of the football world. He had never been the subject of a major magazine article, never appeared on a television commercial. Whenever he was asked to speak, it was always in towns like Vanport, Pennsylvania, and Milton, Massachusetts. Now the telephone never stopped ringing. A dozen agents wanted to sign him. He was named *Sport* magazine's Man of the Year and voted the NFL's Player of the Year. Few people, however, realized that Blanda's success story had taken twenty years to write.

Blanda has to be rated pro football's most successful place-kicker. A glance at the record manual confirms his pre-eminence. Yet in terms of the impact he had on the kicking game and on pro football, in general, Blanda has to take a back seat to Lou Groza, who joined the Cleveland Browns in 1945. Groza was a "pure" kicker, and one of the first. Blanda would beat you in the blink of an eye, but he might do it with a pass as well as a kick. Groza's one specialty is confirmed by his nickname; he was known as "The Toe."

Groza was a big man, indeed, an imposing man —6-foot-3, 245. When he tucked his chin to his chest, started his huge body forward, and powered the heavy leg with its massive thigh into the ball, he seemed capable of kicking it out of sight. Yet Groza was quick to admit that power wasn't his forte. "It's timing," he said. "Size doesn't really make a difference."

When Groza retired in 1967, he ranked as pro football's all-time scoring leader with 1,608 points, a total Blanda exceeded in 1971. Five times Groza led the NFL in field goals, a record that still stands. Another of Groza's records that has stood up is the 88.5 field-goal percentage he attained in 1953. He was successful on 23 of 26 attempts that season, including a stretch where he booted 12 in a row.

Groza was born and brought up in Martins Ferry, Ohio, a grimy industrial town on the Ohio River about sixty miles south and west of Pittsburgh. Dark-haired, strong, and with good size, he was the next to the youngest of four boys. The sports they played varied with the seasons and Lou was never sure whether football or basketball was his favorite. Baseball was a distant third.

Frank, one of Lou's older brothers, place-kicked for Martins Ferry High School, and when Lou decided to become a kicker Frank agreed to coach him. Since the field they used had no goal posts, they used instead telephone wires strung at one end of the field. By the time he entered his sophomore year, Lou was already a skilled kicker.

During his junior and senior years, Lou was the team's star. He still remembers one game. Rugged Blair High was the opposition. Lou had missed two conversion attempts and as the game entered the final quarter, Blair High led, 14–12. Then the coach sent Lou in to try a field goal.

His delight turned to dismay when the snap sailed over his head. Lou retrieved the ball and churned his way through the opposition for a 4-yard gain, which earned the team a first down.

Three running plays failed and again Lou was sent in for another field-goal attempt. The ball was on the 25. This time the pass from center was good. So was Lou's kick, and Martins Ferry won, 15–14.

Groza lumbers forward with an errant snap.

Lou was also a standout basketball player, leading Martins Ferry to the state championship during his senior year. He won ten letters in all, and his studies were no problem for him. College coaches and scouts flooded into Martins Ferry from every part of the country.

Paul Brown, coach at Ohio State University, had heard of Lou's exploits, and sent an assistant to Martins Ferry to offer Lou a full scholarship and a campus job that paid $50 a month. "It wasn't the fanciest offer but it was reasonable," Groza was to say later. He accepted it.

When Lou enrolled at Ohio State in the fall of 1942, World War II was blazing. Although the Buckeye freshman team played only an abbreviated three-game schedule that fall, Lou managed to make a stunning impression with his long and accurate kicks. Then he went into the Army.

Paul Brown was one of the people whom Lou had impressed the most. When Brown left Ohio State and began organizing a new professional team in Cleveland, he made up his mind to sign Groza. He wrote to him regularly and sent him equipment. "Keep practicing," Brown's letters urged. When Groza was sent overseas to the Philippines, a shipment of footballs soon followed.

When the war ended and Lou received his discharge, he hurried to the Cleveland training camp at Bowling Green, Ohio. Officials at Ohio State were embittered because Groza, following Brown's urgings, had decided to forsake college for a career in pro football. Lou was eager to get started in the pros because of the delay caused by his years of military service, and besides he planned to finish college in the off-season—which he did.

Not only was the Cleveland team brand-new, so was the entire league. Known as the All-America Football Conference, it was the brainchild of Arch Ward, a Chicago newspaperman. Owners of NFL teams derided the enterprise, calling it "a bush league."

However, there was nothing second-rate about the Cleveland team—the Browns, as they were to be known. Groza, too, quickly established his capability. A few days after training camp opened, a Cleveland newspaper reporter wrote, "The best show here takes place after regular practice is over. That's when Lou Groza kicks."

When league play began, Groza continued to awe the newspapermen and the fans. The Browns made their debut against a team called the Miami Hurricanes, and blew them out of the stadium, 44–0. Groza contributed three field goals and five extra points. Three field goals in a game was extraordinary for the time. In 1946, Ted Fritsch led the NFL in field goals with nine, and in 1947, seven was the best anyone could do.

Some of Groza's success has to be credited to the scientific methods he used. He liked to take a starting stance precisely 72 inches from the ball, so his holder, Don Greenwood, improvised a piece of tape, 72 inches in length and two inches wide, with a crosspiece at one end which formed the letter T. The T was placed down at the spot the ball was to be held; Lou then lined up at the other end.

The tape and the crosspiece were only one aspect of Groza's methodological approach to place-kicking. Later he and Ernie Godfrey, who had coached Lou at Ohio State, wrote and published a handbook titled "The Art and Technique of Place Kicking," which contained page after page of thoughtful advice.

"As accuracy develops you will use the same cleat marks on the left foot," was one bit of counsel. "You will dig the same holes. These are signs of perfection." Another paragraph read: "If the kicker sees the ball before it crosses the goal post, he is looking up too soon."

Beginning in 1948, Groza also started playing left tackle for the Browns. He liked the idea of playing on a full-time basis. Earlier he had complained to Paul Brown, "I'm a kicker. I want to be a football player."

The All-America Football Conference operated for four years, and every year the Browns won the championship. Still, they were hooted at as being "cheesecake champs" by NFL supporters. In 1950, the Browns were taken into the NFL and fans looked forward to the opportunity of being able to establish the Browns' real worth.

Cleveland managed to handle NFL competition without great difficulty. Although they didn't win with quite the regularity that they had in the old AAFC, they won the title in the NFL's American Conference, which led them to play the Los Angeles Rams for the league crown. The game set the stage for the most important kick of Groza's career.

As snow flurries swirled through Cleveland's Municipal Stadium and a biting wind chilled the 30,000 fans, the Rams rolled to a 28–27 lead with slightly more than two minutes remaining. Unable to move the ball, Los Angeles was forced to punt, and Bob Waterfield sent the ball deep into Cleveland territory. Cliff Lewis made the catch and stepped out of bounds on the Browns' 32-yard line.

One minute and 48 seconds were left as quarterback Otto Graham led the Cleveland offensive unit out onto the field. Graham, unable to find a receiver, ran with the ball and got 14 yards. Then he hit on a pass to Rex Bumgardner. "Go! Go! Go!" the Cleveland fans were screaming.

Graham connected with Dub Jones for 16 yards and with Bumgardner again for 12. It was first down on the Rams' 11-yard line. Now cries of "Groza! Groza!" came from the stands. On the next play, Graham took the snap from center and ran parallel to the line of scrimmage until he was

Sporting News
Financial News

CLEVELAND PLAIN DEALER

Stage and Screen
Classified Ads

MAin 1-4500

CLEVELAND, MONDAY, DECEMBER 25, 1950

49

Groza's Field Goal Is Signal for Celebration

This headline referred to the NFL title game in 1950, but it could have been applied frequently during Groza's long career.

squarely in front of the uprights, then dropped to the ground. All was now in readiness for "The Toe."

The crowd sent up a thunderous roar of approval as Groza trotted out onto the field. He got set without showing the slightest emotion. The pass from center was true. The holder put it down quickly. Groza stepped forward and hit it squarely. Perfect!

In the jubilant Cleveland dressing room, Groza was the center of attention. His teammates hugged him and clapped him on the back.

"Were you nervous?" a reporter asked.

Groza smiled. "I don't get nervous when I kick," he said.

Groza has one claim to fame that other kickers don't have, at least kickers of the present day. He once scored a touchdown. It happened on a snow-filled December afternoon at Griffith Stadium in

Washington in 1950. Quarterback Otto Graham was having a brilliant day, and his pinpoint passing had boosted the Browns into a 38–21 lead. Groza's contributions included a 12-yard field goal and five extra points and, of course, he had also labored at tackle, pass-blocking for Graham and helping to open up holes for the running backs, Marion Motley and Dub Jones.

As the game entered its final minutes, Graham brought the Bears downfield once more. With the ball on the Washington 23-yard line, Cleveland broke from the huddle and into a spread formation. Graham took the snap and darted back, then cocked his arm and searched downfield. He spotted a man all alone on the Washington 10-yard line— Groza. Graham fired and the ball hit big Lou on his orange number 76. He clasped it to his chest and lumbered into the end zone without a hand touching him.

When football historians recount the significant plays of 1950, they usually overlook Groza's touchdown catch. You can't blame them. His own exploits help to obscure it. The very next week

63

Gino Cappelletti

Groza kicked two field goals, the deciding factor in the Browns' 8–3 win over the Giants for the championship of the NFL's American Conference. And the week after that he booted the 16-yard field goal that gave the Browns their 30–28 win over the Rams and the pro football title. Lou never scored another touchdown because he never had another chance. Before the next season began, a rule change was put into effect which stated that tackles were ineligible as pass receivers.

In the years that followed, the Browns remained the dominant force in professional football, winning their conference or league title every year through 1955. Groza was their scoring leader every year, and he continued to be until the great Jimmy Brown joined the team and began scoring touchdowns at a record rate.

In the latter years of his career, Groza's accumulating paunch began to slow him down and there were rumors that the Browns were going to let him go. But while the coaches had no trouble finding trimmer kickers, they couldn't find a better one. Finally, a week before the 1968 season opened, Groza stepped aside in favor of twenty-three-year-old Don Cockroft. At the time he retired, "The Toe" held 10 NFL and 24 team records.

In all of pro football history, only one other player has scored points with the frequency that Groza and Blanda scored them—Gino Cappelletti. When he gave up his job with the New England Patriots just before the opening of the 1971 season, Cappelletti ranked third on the NFL's list of "Most Points, Lifetime." He owned the American League's career scoring record with 1,130 points, and the record for most points scored in a single season with 155. He captured the AFL's season scoring title a record five times.

These achievements have to be regarded in a special light, for Cappelletti was not blessed with an abundance of natural talent. What he did have was desire. "Gino was as diligent an athlete as any player I've ever seen," Patriot coach Mike Holovak once said. "He had an intense determination. He had ability, too, although he wasn't greatly endowed. But he made himself exceptional by working at it."

Cappelletti's grit was apparent during his college years at Minnesota. In the first quarter of a 7–7 Minnesota-Iowa game, Cappelletti, a member of the defensive squad, was on the bench when a crucial third-down play came up. Gino walked over to coach Wes Fesler and said, "Coach, if we don't make it, let me try a field goal."

"Are you crazy?" said Fesler. "Go and sit down." What made the suggestion "crazy" was the fact that Minnesota hadn't tried a field goal in years; they hadn't even practiced one.

When the third-down play failed, Fesler turned and stared at Gino. Finally he said, "Go in and kick it."

When Cappelletti announced the play in the huddle, his teammates started laughing. But Gino made it, and with plenty of room to spare. Minnesota went on to win, 17–7. It was the first field goal Cappelletti had ever attempted in collegiate competition.

His determination is what got Cappelletti into pro football in the first place. He had just passed his twenty-sixth birthday in 1960 when he realized that his life was at a crossroads. He had completed a two-year stint with the Army and also had wound up his football career, which involved two seasons as a quarterback for the Sarnia Imperials in the Ontario Rugby Football Union. Now he was tending bar at a tavern in Minneapolis, which he owned in partnership with Bob McNamara, a former teammate at the University of Minnesota.

This was the time that the American Football League was being organized, and coach Lou Saban of the Boston Patriots (they became the New England Patriots in 1971) arrived in Minneapolis in search of playing talent. Saban signed McNamara and several other Minnesota stars. But Cappelletti, a defensive back for the team, wasn't even contacted.

He made up his mind to at least win a chance to try out. He telephoned Saban's hotel but too late; the coach had checked out. He then called the airport, only to be told the coach's flight had left ten minutes before. Gino then obtained Saban's home phone number in Illinois and began calling him there. Once he finally got Saban on the line, he offered to pay his own expenses if the coach would invite him to training camp. "You can use me as a defensive back, a kicker, or both," said Gino. Saban said he'd have to think about it, that he'd call him back. Gino waited two months before the call came.

"I had just about given up," he says. "I figured I had been given the brushoff. Then the call came. Saban said that if I could make the team, they'd give me a minimum contract. I was so excited that I forgot to ask how much the minimum was."

Later Gino found out it was $7,500. But any amount would have been appreciated. "I don't think I had as much as $50 in my pocket when I arrived at camp," he once recalled. "The lock on my suitcase was broken and I had to tie a belt around it to keep it closed."

Cappelletti was one of the more than 300 candidates that passed through the Patriots' training camp that summer. Ninety per cent failed to make the team and Cappelletti himself came close to being cut several times. Aware of how precarious his situation was, Cappelletti began to practice as a pass receiver. Mike Holovak, the team's offensive backfield coach at the time, encouraged Gino to keep working at the position, and he helped to tutor him.

Cappelletti's first field-goal attempt for the Patriots was one of the most important of his career. It came in the first period of the first American Football League game ever played. The Denver Broncos were the opposition. The scene was Boston University Field, a night game.

The Patriots had taken the opening kickoff and marched downfield. The drive stalled on the Denver 35-yard line and Cappelletti was sent in.

"I tried to be cool and calm but I couldn't," he recalled. "I was too nervous, too excited. And when the ball came back I froze. I couldn't move. The ball was down and I was just standing there looking at it like a bad dream. Suddenly I lunged at it and kicked it. And it was good.

"I thought about that kick many times in the years afterward. If I had missed it, I might have been cut from the team. Lots of guys in those years made just one costly mistake and it was all over."

Cappelletti began his career as a pass receiver in the final game of the season, catching a 28-yarder. In the years that followed, his exploits as a kicker usually overshadowed his pass receiving, yet he won a reputation for his sure-handedness and his ability to get open in pressure situations. Over his career, the 6-foot, 190-pound Cappelletti caught 282 passes good for 42 touchdowns and 4,575 yards.

Cappelletti the kicker resembled Cappelletti the pass receiver in that he always seemed to be at his best in clutch moments. In 1961, his second year with the team, he kicked a field goal against the Dallas Texans at the same instant the final gun went off, to give the Patriots an 18–17 victory.

Another time, with the Patriots facing the Hous-

Toe at the ready, Cappelletti awaits the call to action.

ton Oilers at Fenway Park in Boston, Cappelletti was sent in to try a 41-yard field goal with one second to play. Making it would give the Patriots an important win. Just as the teams lined up, the Oilers, in an effort to rattle Gino, called a timeout. The strategy failed to work and the kick was perfect. The ecstatic Boston fans surged from the stands, picked up Cappelletti, and carried him from the field.

In the AFL's 1963 Eastern Division play-off, played in arctic temperatures on a frozen field at Buffalo's War Memorial Stadium, Cappelletti was never better. Wearing a sneaker on his left foot for traction and his size 10E kicking shoe on the right, he didn't miss once, booting four field goals and two conversions for the Patriots' 26–8 win.

During his rookie season with the Patriots, Gino happened to read how Bob Waterfield of the Rams had once kicked five field goals in a game. It had happened in 1951 and was still the record. "If I could do that," said Cappelletti, "I'd be the happiest guy in the world."

Late in September, 1964, against the New York Jets, Gino kicked four field goals. Reporters clustered around him after the game. "Some day I'll go Waterfield one better," he said. "Some day it will be six. I have a feeling it will come soon."

It's not likely that Cappelletti realized how soon. It happened the very next week. The record, achieved at the expense of the Denver Broncos, came on kicks of 11, 30, 16, 48, 15 and 18 yards. The 48-yarder was a personal record for Gino at the time. When the AFL merged with the NFL in 1969, the record of six field goals for a game was still on the books, although it had been equalled once by Jim Turner.

Gino's determination to succeed was never limited to his career as a player. It touched every aspect of his life. He was nervous and insecure as a rookie, and after one of his early speaking engagements a Boston sportswriter described him as "terrible." But by working at it, Cappelletti made himself skilled, and within two years became one of the Patriots' most sought-after speakers. That's not the end of the story. After he retired as an active player, Gino became a radio announcer, broadcasting the Patriot games for New England fans.

THE BEST TODAY

It's generally agreed that field-goal kickers are in the headlines nowadays much more than they were a few years ago. One reason for this is Tom Dempsey of the Philadelphia Eagles. A single kick of his was all it took to increase the eminence of field-goal specialists in general and make Dempsey a standout figure among his peers.

The time: November 8, 1970. The place: Tulane Stadium in New Orleans. The Detroit Lions lead the New Orleans Saints, Dempsey's team at the time, 17–16. Two seconds remain.

Into the game comes Dempsey to try a never-before-attempted 63-yard field goal. His head down, Dempsey takes two short steps, then explodes the ball toward the Lion goal. He lifts his head to watch but the mass of players in front of him obscures his view of the ball, which clears the crossbar by inches. Suddenly Dempsey sees the referee thrust both hands into the air and he hears the huge crowd roar hysterically. He realizes that he has won the game for the Saints. Then it dawns on him that he also has happened to kick the ball 63 yards, seven yards farther than the previous longest field goal in pro football history.

It was the play of the season, and not simply because of the distance involved. (Dempsey kicked from the New Orleans 37-yard line, which is three yards farther back than the kickoff point.) Demp-

Tom Dempsey

69

sey was born handicapped, with half a right foot, his kicking foot, and only a stub for a right hand.

But Dempsey, who stands 6-foot-1 and weighs 270, does not consider his deformity a handicap. He was never allowed to. Born in Milwaukee in 1941, Dempsey was brought up in southern California. His parents always made him feel that he could do anything anybody else could do. He once told an interviewer: "Anytime I'd say, 'I can't do that,' my dad would thump me one and say, 'There's no such word as *can't.*' I grew up believing that."

The philosophy paid dividends. Dempsey was an All Star first baseman in Little League and, like most California youngsters, he surfed. At Palomar Junior College, he wrestled, played defensive end, and occasionally place-kicked, shoeless, with tape wrapped around his foot.

He tried out with San Diego in 1968 but the Chargers eventually dropped him because they had Dennis Partee, a place-kicker who could also punt. Sid Gillman, then coach of the Chargers, told Dempsey that he would be more successful if he wore a shoe. In fact, Gillman had a special shoe designed for him. Made in part of fiberglass, it looked like a conventional shoe. Dempsey found it to be too heavy and sometimes it hurt his foot.

But Dempsey realized that wearing a shoe was a good idea and during the off-season he worked with a manufacturer of orthopedic shoes to develop

On display at the Hall of Fame, this is the shoe Dempsey used in booting his record 63-yarder.

one of suitable size and weight. After trying more than a dozen different designs, they hit on a model that was comfortable to wear and seemed to get the job done. About 6½ inches in length, it was shaped like Dempsey's foot and offered a flat, rectangular kicking surface about the size of a bubble-gum card. This is the type of shoe Dempsey wears today and it is similar to the one he used for his record kick.

After Dempsey was dropped by the Chargers, he tried out with the New Orleans Saints, winning his job in practice sessions and preseason competition. Coach Tom Fears settled on Dempsey because of the way he boomed the ball high and deep on kickoffs.

Dempsey was sensational as a rookie, kicking 22 field goals and scoring 99 points. He was named to the NFL's All Star team and played in the Pro Bowl.

Problems developed the next year, however. Dempsey tore a hip muscle during the preseason schedule, which reduced his effectiveness. When the team got off to a slow start, Coach Fears was released. Dempsey and the new coach, J.D. Roberts, did not get along well.

"We never hit it off," says Dempsey. "He had his way and I had mine. He didn't understand that a kicker has to be left alone to work out his problems. He just wants to kick, kick, kick—like a golfer practicing shots.

"When you get right down to it, there are few men qualified to coach a kicker. George Blanda and Lou Groza, I'd listen to." The name "J. D. Roberts" never made Dempsey's list.

The conflict reached a showdown early in 1971. Dempsey, hailed on the winter banquet circuit for his heroic 63-yard boot the season before, showed up at training camp overweight. "Instead of lifting weights," Dempsey admitted, "I had been lifting too many knives and forks. I wasn't in good shape." After Dempsey missed seven of eight field-goal attempts during the 1971 preseason schedule, Roberts released him.

Dempsey then started making telephone calls but only the Eagles bothered to call him back. After signing with the club, he was activated for the tenth game of the season. In the five games he played, Dempsey was successful on 12 of 17 field-goal tries, which gave him a .706 average, the NFL's best in 1971. His successful attempts included kicks of 50, 52, and 54 yards, which matched Jan Stenerud of Kansas City for the season's longest.

The Philadelphia coaches rate Dempsey a scoring threat anytime the team has the ball within 50 or 60 yards of the opposition goal, depending on wind conditions. Then Dempsey gets up from his seat on the bench, dons his helmet, and begins a nervous watch, tossing wisps of grass into the air to get a reading on the wind, checking the clock, conferring with his holder and coaches. "Field goal team!" a coach yells out, and seconds later Dempsey and his colleagues take the field.

Dempsey's approach is smooth and unhurried. Head down, he thumps the ball toward his target. His follow-through is short, reaching only to about waist level.

In some quarters Dempsey has a reputation as a fine long-distance kicker but is believed to have problems at short range. He calls this evaluation "nonsense."

"One day," he says, "I happened to miss a couple of short ones—everyone does—and because

I have the ability to kick long, some writer decided that *all* I could do was kick long." He points out that in 1971 he was successful on six of seven attempts inside the 30-yard line.

How does pressure affect Dempsey? He thrives on it. "I like the pressure of being a field-goal kicker," he says. "I love it, in fact.

"I enjoy the feel that the whole game is mine. I'm the man who has to do the job for the whole team. It's the kind of experience that you don't get often in life."

While Dempsey's ability to be consistent has been questioned, one man who has never been doubted in this regard is Jan Stenerud of the Kansas City Chiefs. He rates as the most efficient kicker of recent times. During a period from November 2 to December 7, 1969, Stenerud booted 16 consecutive field goals, a pro record no other kicker has approached. (Cleveland's Lou Groza and Detroit's Bobby Layne, each of whom kicked 12 consecutive field goals during the 1950's, are the runners-up.)

A soccer-style specialist, Stenerud is no slouch when it comes to distance kicking. He twice kicked field goals of 54 yards during his AFL days. The league record, held by George Blanda, is only one

Perfectly balanced, Dempsey tries a 50-yard field goal during warm-up session.

Jan Stenerud

yard more. At Montana State University, Stenerud set an NCAA record by connecting on a 59-yarder in 1965. He set another collegiate record the next year by scoring 82 points.

Besides the plaques, trophies, and record-book recognition, Stenerud can point to another tribute earned by his skilled right toe, or, more accurately, instep. It's a painted sign that hangs in the stands behind one of the Kansas City goal posts and proclaims "Stenerud's Roost." That's where the fans want him to put kickoffs.

From Festund in Norway, Stenerud began playing organized soccer when he was about eight years old, and although he made better-than-average progress in the sport it wasn't his main interest. Ski jumping was. At twenty, he finished sixth in a national junior ski-jumping tournament. "That meant," he says, "that there were only five youngsters better than me in the country. And in Norway, remember, every boy who is old enough to walk also skis and wants to be a skier, so the competition is rough. Another thing, you usually don't reach your peak until you're in your late twenties."

Stenerud's talent as a skier became known to Tor Fageraas, another Norwegian, who was attending Montana State. He wrote to Stenerud and asked him whether he would be interested in coming to Montana State on a ski scholarship, and Jan accepted the offer.

The ski team worked out on a track near the football team's practice field. Stenerud got to know many of the football players, and one day during his junior year they asked him to try place-kicking. He attempted to kick the ball with his toe but could hardly get it off the ground. Switching to the soccer technique, he put the ball through the uprights several times without any difficulty.

His friends, eager to see how far he could kick, kept moving him back. "That first day I kicked a 50-yard field goal," Stenerud recalls. "But I didn't know I had done well because I didn't know enough about football to know whether a kick of that distance was any good."

When the football coach heard about the incident, he convinced Jan to join the team. Stenerud soon developed such a fondness for what he then called "the crazy game of football" that ski jumping became of secondary importance to him. Even though he won two NCAA ski-jumping championships during college, he was much better known for his skill as a place-kicker, and when he graduated he was drafted by both the Atlanta Falcons of the NFL and the Chiefs, then an AFL team.

Stenerud quickly decided to choose the Chiefs. "Hank Stram really impressed me," he says. "He just didn't talk about signing. He talked about kicking and he knew what he was talking about."

Some kickers analyze their stance, approach, and the kick itself down to the finest detail. Not Stenerud. "I don't want to study myself too closely or get too technical," he says, "because I'm afraid that would hurt more than do good.

"When trying for a field goal, I line up almost the same way every time, but I don't really count the steps. I'm watching the ball, concentrating on that.

"The ball usually hooks to the left when I kick. If there's a wind from the right, then I really have to compensate. Sometimes I have to aim the ball to the right of the right goal post and then hope it hooks in."

What is Stenerud's "secret"? What has made him one of the outstanding place-kickers of the 1970's? "I don't think it takes a great, strong leg," he says. "It's just quickness, a certain snap, and the way you hit the ball. It comes naturally."

Stenerud has some heady football memories—like the 1970 Super Bowl in which he booted three quick field goals to give the Chiefs a 9–0 lead over the favored Minnesota Vikings, enabling Kansas City to dominate the game and to win it with relative ease. There was an afternoon in Buffalo when Stenerud attempted five field goals and made five. And there are the countless times he has come into a game in a clutch situation and delivered. "He's a

Stenerud ranks as perhaps the most consistent of all soccer stylists.

Many of the 50,734 spectators at Kansas City's Municipal Stadium that unseasonably warm afternoon, and millions who watched on television, would call it the greatest game ever played. One thing is certain: it *was* the longest game ever played. At the end of regulation time, the score was tied, 24–24. The sudden-death period that followed was scoreless. Finally, at 7:40 of the second overtime period, it ended.

guaranteed three points," Coach Hank Stram has said.

But there is one memory that is a nightmare. It involves a game on Christmas Day, 1971, a showdown struggle between the Chiefs and the Miami Dolphins for the championship of the American Football Conference. The winner would go to the Super Bowl.

Stenerud's opportunity came in the fourth quarter. On the kickoff following a Dolphin touchdown, the Chief's Ed Podolak took the ball straight up the middle. At midfield he swerved to his left and then streaked down the sideline past open-mouthed players on the Dolphin bench. For an instant it seemed as if he would go all the way, but he was jounced out of bounds at the Miami 22-yard line. One minute, 25 seconds remained.

Hank Stram ordered three running plays to use up time. With 31 seconds left, and the ball on the Miami 31-yard line, Stenerud trotted out onto the field. The Miami bench was surrounded in gloom, the players staring at the ground. For Stenerud, a 31-yard field goal was a piece of cake. In his five years with the Chiefs, he had tried 86 field goals from the 31-yard line in; he had made 74 of them.

There was no wind. As for the pressure, Stenerud had twice won games that season in the final ten seconds.

The snap was perfect. The hold was perfect. Stenerud planted his left foot, then swept his right foot through. When he looked up, his heart sank, for the ball was spinning off to the right. It went outside the right upright by about six inches.

Without waiting to see the referee's signal confirming the catastrophe, Stenerud turned and trudged from the field. Hank Stram was waiting to meet him. "It's all right," said Stram. "It's all right."

"No," said Stenerud, his voice barely audible. "It's not all right."

Stenerud got a chance to redeem himself in the first overtime period, with the ball on the Miami 35-yard line. But the snap from center was high and the Dolphins' Nick Buoniconti blocked the kick and the ball rolled dead. The Chiefs' chances died with it. The next scoring opportunity belonged to Garo Yepremian, the Dolphins' short (5-foot-7) and balding soccer specialist.

With three minutes gone in the second overtime period, Miami took over the ball on their own 30-yard line. Jim Kiick and Larry Csonka, the Dolphin's high-powered running backs, took turns carrying, and five plays later the ball rested on the Kansas City 30-yard line.

The crowd was tense and silent as Yepremian came out onto the field. "Keep your eyes on the ball and make sure you follow through," he was saying to himself. He knew if he did that the big Kansas City linemen would not be able to block it.

No one blocked it. It cleared the desperate hands and floated over the bar and between the uprights. The Dolphin players leaped into the air, their arms raised in triumph. Yepremian held his fists high as he raced from the field to be mobbed by his teammates.

Ironically, Yepremian, who was born in Larnaca, Cyprus, had been challenging Stenerud's status as the game's premier place-kicker all sea-

Garo Yepremian

son long. During 1971, he kicked 28 field goals and converted 33 points after touchdown, a total of 117 points. No one in the NFL had done better than that. Three times his kicks had won games for the Dolphins.

Being the No. 1 kicker in football was always an ambition of Yepremian. When he signed with the Detroit Lions as a free agent in 1966, he asked for jersey No. 1. "It's because I wanted to be the No. 1 kicker," he says. It's the number he wears today.

Yepremian is extremely accurate on any kick up to 50 yards, and from inside the 40-yard line he's deadly. He takes two quick steps, then punches the ball with his left foot. There's little follow-through.

"If you hit the right spot, you don't need power," he says. "It's timing. When I try to hit the ball with all my strength, I kill it. The ball sails off to the side like a dying duck."

The confidence that he's developed in the past few years has also been a factor in his success. "When I was with the Lions, I had a coach who always found something wrong when I missed," Garo recalls. "He'd say it was overswing, a bad angle, or something. But now I have experience, I know enough not to listen to all the advice I get. When somebody tells me what I'm doing wrong, I just say, 'Thank you, very much,' and kick the way I always kick."

Like other standout kickers, Yepremian seems unbothered by pressure. He seldom allows for the wind and is able to ignore towering linemen. "I just try to kick it straight through the middle," he says.

In light of all he's accomplished, it seems implausible that Garo never even heard of American

pro football until he was well into his teens. As a boy growing up in Cyprus, his ambition was to be a professional soccer player. His father hired one of the best coaches in Europe to tutor him. Garo would kick a soccer ball against the side of a building for hours without letup, trying to make the ball burst. When it did, his father would buy him a new one.

When Garo was fifteen, the family moved to England and he went to work as a cutter in a clothing factory. In his spare time he played for an English semipro soccer team. One day Garo received a letter from his brother, Krikor, who was captain of the soccer team at the University of Indiana. "Buy a football and start practicing," the letter said.

Garo came to the United States and entered Butler University in Indianapolis. He stayed six weeks, practicing his kicking and learning the rules of football. The Detroit Lions gave him a tryout and then signed him. The following Saturday he played in the first American football game he had ever seen.

Yepremian's size, or lack of it, and his unfamiliarity with football made him the butt of countless jokes. The Lions kidded him that he wore No. 1 on his jersey because his chest wasn't big enough for any other number.

Yepremian tends his kicking toe.

Tackle Alex Karras, the team's chief needler, had Garo in mind when, in describing soccer-style kickers, he said: "These guys sit there on the bench and then come in for a few seconds and kick, and then they run around squealing, 'I keek a touchdown. I keek a touchdown.' "

Yepremian didn't do badly as a rookie, although he failed to finish among the scoring leaders. One afternoon he was sublime, kicking six field goals, almost one-half of his season's total, in a game against the Minnesota Vikings. Six field goals in a game was the league record at the time. Someone asked Minnesota coach Norm Van Brocklin what he planned to do about Yepremian in the future. "Tighten the immigration laws," Van Brocklin snapped.

There was a coaching change the next year and Garo found himself out of favor. Many an afternoon that season he never left his seat on the bench, and he ended up scoring only 28 points.

The season that followed was even worse. Unable to win his job back with the Lions, he spent part of the season as a place-kicker for the Michigan Arrows, a minor league team. To support himself, he designed, made, and sold neckties, which later caused sportswriters to observe that Garo was a tie-maker off the field and often a tie-breaker on it.

The turning point in Garo's career came in 1970 when Don Shula, the new coach of the Miami Dolphins, agreed to look him over. In the second game of the season, Garo kicked 31- and 42-yard field goals, and the following week he booted a 47-yarder in a tropical downpour. Soon after, he was named Miami's No. 1 kicker.

He has since become one of the most popular of the Dolphin players. "Garo! Garo! Garo!" the fans chant over and over at Miami home games. Autograph seekers besiege him everywhere he goes, and after a home game he's almost always the last player out of the parking lot. Youngsters are constantly coming to his home to ask for inscribed pictures. "Maybe the reason youngsters like me so much," says Garo, "is because I'm more their size."

If Garo has any complaints, it's that he sometimes finds football boring, especially the practice sessions. He still doesn't fully understand the game, and though he sometimes plays the role of a wide receiver during defensive drills, he spends a good deal of time standing around and watching. To break the monotony, he sometimes tries to hit the goal posts with his place kicks.

One other of the game's soccer stylists must be mentioned. His name is Chester Marcol. He joined the Green Bay Packers in 1972 as a twenty-two-year-old rookie. One day his achievements may equal those of Garo Yepremian and Jan Stenerud.

At Hillsdale College in Michigan, Chester earned a national reputation by once kicking a record 62-yard field goal, and he kicked eight

others of 50 yards or more. In one game he attempted a 77-yarder; it was short by five yards. He also established a college record of 105 consecutive field goals.

Marcol learned how to kick during his boyhood in Opole, Poland. He was known as Czeslaw Marcol then, not Chester. After his father died in 1964, his mother brought the family to Imlay City, Michigan, to live with relatives.

Chester's gym teacher at Imlay City High School discovered his kicking talent and introduced him to the football coach. After graduation, Chester enrolled at Hillsdale as a foreign student taking English as a foreign language. Now an American citizen, he speaks English fluently.

Marcol, who is 6-foot-1 and 190, also punts. He averaged 48.2 yards on 52 punts in college. The Packers used one of their highest draft choices to land him.

Green Bay captured its third consecutive league title in 1967, but the next year the team lost more games than it won and then one mediocre season followed another. Some football experts equate the team's poor showing with Vince Lombardi's resignation as head coach. Others say that the failure of the kicking game was a major factor, that many losses could have been converted into victories with

Wearing uniform of the College All Stars, Chester Marcol swoops in on a field-goal try.

a field goal at the appropriate time. Whatever the reason, the Packers are counting on young Chester Marcol to help the team regain its winning tradition.

Toe-kicker Fred Cox of the Minnesota Vikings is a prime example of what a kicker can contribute in helping to establish a team as a consistent winner. Up until 1972, when Fran Tarkenton took over as a quarterback and energized the Minnesota offense, Cox was the man the Vikings depended on to put points on the scoreboard. Take 1971, for example. The Vikings scored 245 points; 91 of them, slightly more than 40 per cent, were Cox's. Since his rookie year of 1963, Cox has led the league in field goals three times, in scoring twice, and in recent years he has been moving steadily up the list of the game's top ten scorers. He's not yet a threat to George Blanda or Lou Groza, but at his present pace he'll supplant Gino Cappelletti as the No. 3 man some winter afternoon in 1974 or 1975.

Perhaps the most glittering evidence of Cox's consistency is his current string of 126 consecutive games scoring, the NFL record. The only extra-point attempts he's ever missed are those that have been blocked.

When he graduated from the University of Pittsburgh in 1962, Cox was signed by the Cleve-

Fred Cox

land Browns as a kicker and running back. It's easy to understand why the 5-foot-10, 210-pound Cox didn't stay there very long. The Browns had Lou Groza to do their kicking and the great Jimmy Brown their ball carrying. Cox was traded to the Vikings before the season began.

He failed to impress anyone at the Minnesota training camp, and the club released him. "You've got good potential as a kicker," he was told by a Minnesota official. "We'll give you a call next spring."

Figuring that he had been brushed off, Cox headed home sadly. He began making plans to become a school teacher. But the next spring, the call did come. "How soon can you get to training camp?" Cox was asked. "When's the next plane?" he answered.

"It was between me and Mike Eischeid at training camp that summer," Cox recalls. "Since I had been in camp the year before, I was given the first chance in our opening preseason game. I was lucky and I kicked five field goals."

Cox went on to have a fine rookie season, accounting for 75 points. He also handled the punting. "I was on top of the world," he says.

The next summer misfortune struck: Cox developed a serious back ailment. The pain was so severe that he couldn't raise his leg to kick; he could hardly walk, in fact. As part of the therapy, doctors encased his body in ice. The treatment was

Cox provides scoring punch for Vikings.

82

successful and that fall he had a banner season.

When Cox kicked 43 extra points and 26 field goals in 1969, the 121 points he scored set a record for "pure" kickers. The very next season, he topped it, kicking 35 extra points and 30 field goals—125 points. (He hasn't done any punting since his rookie year.)

"The most important things in kicking," Cox says, "are strong legs and stronger concentration. It also helps to be a little tense, especially on the longer attempts."

Cox cites Viking defensive back Paul Krause as the "best holder I've ever had because of his quick-ness. The longer I see the ball on the ground, the better my chances of being successful. I never look at the center. I'm looking at the spot on the ground that Paul has pointed out to me. Then I catch sight of the ball at the top of my vision and I start to move. By the time he catches the ball, I've started forward."

Jim Turner of the Denver Broncos is Cox's rival as the game's foremost toe-kicker. Turner used to be a member of the Jets and when the New Yorkers went to the Super Bowl in January, 1969, and beat the Baltimore Colts, "The Tank," as his teammates used to call him, played a vital role. He kicked a record 34 field goals that season, a figure that no one—not Jan Stenerud or Fred Cox—has ever come close to.

In the Super Bowl game itself, Turner's square toe was responsible for 10 of the Jets' 16 points. "Super Toe wasn't less than Super Joe Namath," said New York *Post* columnist Milt Gross.

Turner's style is a bit unusual in that he jabs the ball, punches it, with almost no follow-through. This means that he has to hit the ball with greater impact than the average kicker. "With me, it's kind of a jerky thing," he says, "but the moment I hit it I know whether it's going to go far enough. Usually I can tell by the 'pop.'"

Born in Martinez, California, Turner attended high school in nearby Crockett. There he received one of the few coaching tips that he remembers.

Jim Turner

Turner and holder Babe Parilli during Jet practice.

"Don't run at the ball," he was told. At Utah State University, he place-kicked *and* quarterbacked. The fall after he graduated he asked the Jets to give him a tryout. Team officials told him to pay a call on the club's next trip to Oakland. With his brother doing the holding, Turner impressed the coaches enough to earn a contract. It was years, however, before he felt secure in his job. Jet coach Weeb Ewbank was forever appraising free agents, more than a hundred of them, Turner estimates. He had to outduel each one.

In his years with the Jets—he was traded to Denver in 1971—Turner was always quick to credit his holder, Babe Parilli, for much of the success he achieved. Parilli had long experience, having held for Gino Cappelletti of the Patriots during the years he led the AFL in scoring. When Parilli became the Jet holder, he suggested that the spot where the ball was to be placed be moved five inches closer to the center. Parilli had noticed that he often had to spin the ball's laces away from Turner. He figured out that moving up the ball would take a half a revolution less, and thus the laces would always be in proper position.

In recent seasons, Turner has shown that he can kick as well in the rarefied air of Denver as he ever did in gusty Shea Stadium. The Broncos, through 1971, had never had a winning season. The betting is that Jim Turner is going to change that, or at least help to.

The Chiefs' Jerrel Wilson

PUNTING AND PUNTERS

In recent years, or ever since he joined the Kansas City Chiefs in 1963, an eleventh-round draft choice out of the University of Southern Mississippi, Jerrel Wilson, has been pro football's most sensational punter. In the years that he hasn't won a league or conference title, he has come very close.

Wilson, a big man—6-foot-4, 220 pounds—and a natural athlete, attributed his success to a style which called for him to attack the ball, to punish it, on every kick. "I try to put everything I can into every kick," Wilson once said, "my knees, my hips, everything.

"Every time I hit the ball, I try to bust it." By "busting it," Wilson meant just that—exploding the ball, deflating it. That was Wilson's ambition everywhere except when kicking from around the 50-yard line. "Then I try to hang it high," he said. In practice, Wilson punted 100 times a day.

To Wilson, the ideal punt was one that went over the receiver's head. Kansas City coach Hank Stram describes the perfect punt in more specific terms. He wants a punt that is kicked within 1.8 seconds, travels 45 yards or more, and has a "hang time" of 4.5 seconds. "Hang time" means time aloft, how long the ball stays in the air. It's of vital importance. A low, line-drive punt—what Stram calls a "frozen rope"—doesn't give the kicking

team sufficient time to get downfield and cover the return. A long runback is likely to result.

Stram wants his punter to attain these statistics on every kick. He doesn't want him to blast the ball 60 yards one time and only 30 yards the next. "Consistency, that's what we look for," says Stram. "More than anything else, we look for consistency."

Other punters strive for statistics similar to those established by Stram. Ron Widby, who does the punting for the Green Bay Packers, seeks to kick the ball within 2.3 seconds of the time its centered. "It takes about .6 of a second to get back to you and you have to kick it within 1.7 seconds," he says.

A punting coach always carries a stopwatch. He

times the number of seconds between the center's snap and the sound of the kick, and how long the ball is in the air. Parts of seconds are critical. In the fall of 1969, veteran Curley Johnson of the New York Jets was challenged by rookie Steve O'Neal for the job as the team's punter. Day after day they dueled in training camp practice sessions. Ultimately the coaches decided in favor of O'Neal for the job. The two men had kept the ball aloft

Ron Widby shouts encouragement from the sidelines.

for about the same amount of time on each kick and they were about equal as far as punting distance was concerned. But what balanced the scales in O'Neal's favor was his ability to get off his kicks from one-fifth to one-half of a second faster than Johnson.

Television broadcasters and football statisticians always evaluate punts and punters in terms of yardage. But coaches don't nor do the punters themselves. Yardage is only part of the picture. The leading punters in professional football, in terms of yardage, average about 45 yards per kick. But a professional could probably average 60 to 70 yards per kick if distance were the only objective.

Some indication of what might be able to be achieved can be gained from the results of the national "Punt, Pass, and Kick" competition sponsored annually for boys eight to thirteen by the Ford Dealers of America and the National Football League. Punting contestants are judged on the basis of how far each can kick, and in one recent year the thirteen-year-old finalist punted 112 yards, the twelve-year-old, 79 yards, and the eleven-year-old, 90 yards. It's anyone's guess what a professional punter might be able to do if he tried.

Some people say that punters today are less skilled then those of past seasons, and they point to the averages, citing Sammy Baugh of the Washington Redskins, who led the NFL in punting for

four consecutive years beginning in 1940 and set distance records that have never been equalled. But Baugh, like all punters of the time, quick-kicked a good deal, that is, punted on third down when it wasn't expected. His kicks often sailed over the heads of the opposition players and then rolled—and rolled and rolled. Baugh was a great kicker; there can be no doubt of that. But he was not quite as pre-eminent as the record manual indicates.

Passing a football or tucking it to your belly and running with it are done instinctively, but there's not much that's natural about the art of punting. You have to be able to balance on one leg, then swing the other foot into a leather ball that's constructed more for throwing and catching than kicking. It takes plenty of concentration and coordination to be successful.

The matter of balance is extremely important. The punter has to be able to provide a stable base from which to launch the punt, even though the leg swing tends to pull the body off balance.

The late LeRoy Mills, one of punting's most knowledgeable coaches, used to give prospective punters a simple test to check their balance. He would instruct each man to walk forward and back over a straight line which was 50 yards in length.

Steve O'Neal is relaxed as he waits for the center's snap.

Then each was blindfolded and told to walk the line again. Some would go beyond the line before turning; others would turn before reaching the end. Almost all wandered off the course, drifting to either the right or left, and some lost their sense of direction completely. Those in the last named category were advised to try something else besides punting.

Virtually all punters are right-footed, although the Philadelphia Eagles used left-footer Bill Bradley when Tom McNeill, their No. 1 punter, was injured in 1972. Bradley had punted in 1969 for the team, averaging 39.8 yards per kick on 74 kicks. Because the ball spirals from a left-footer's foot in the "wrong" direction, it can be difficult for the return man to handle.

Size doesn't have a great deal to do with it, although most professional punters are six feet tall or taller, and Green Bay's Ron Widby stands 6-foot-4. But on the college teams there are countless successful punters who are of no more than average height and weight.

Strong legs are necessary, but there is a variety of opinions as to how this strength should be built. Most punters speak highly of isometric exercise but there are mixed feelings about weight-lifting. Any such program must be supervised by a specialist in the field.

A punting rarity—*left-footer* Bill Bradley.

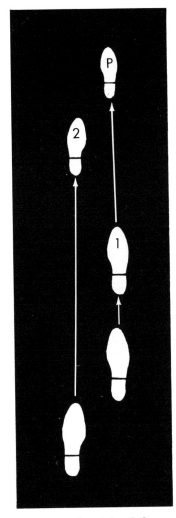

The approach: right, left, punt.

Much more than strong legs are involved in getting a long, high kick. Actually, three movements are involved: (1) the punter's approach—the forward steps he takes, what's called his "linear movement"; (2) the upward swing of the kicking leg from the hip; and (3) the straightening movement of the foreleg as the instep makes contact, what coaches call the "snap."

These three pieces of action are incorporated in the three-step approach, the right foot swinging into the ball on the final step. The punter's stance as he awaits the snap should be comfortable and relaxed.

It's right step, left stride—swing. The first step is relatively short, from 12 to 18 inches in length. The second step (with the left foot) is longer, a full natural step. As the left foot is planted, the punter starts to swing his right foot through. His eyes are glued on the ball.

As the instep of his right foot moves into the ball, the leg straightens with a quick snap. The ball is about knee-level at the moment contact is made. The point of contact is a spot slightly to the rear of the ball's center. The ankle of the kicker must be rigid at contact and toes straight, never curled up.

Follow-through is vital, with the right leg swinging as high as possible. "Don't lift your body completely off the ground," say the instruction books. But it's a piece of advice few pro kickers heed.

Bobby Joe Green's momentum lifts him high above the ground.

Their momentum carries them several inches into the air.

A critical element in every punt is the drop, the release of the ball to the kicking foot. Poor kicks are usually the result of poor drops. Coaches want the drop to be a short one, with the right hand releasing the ball as close as possible to the right foot.

Some kickers want the ball to nose down slightly as it drops; others want a drop that's perfectly flat. What no one wants is a ball that drops nose up. This type strikes the kicker's instep tail-end first and an end-over-end kick is the result.

A common failing among beginner punters is forgetting to lock the ankle tightly as the ball is kicked. When you lock your ankle, the forward part of your foot turns down. This causes the ball, once it's reached the peak of its trajectory, to nose over and keep going. But when the ankle isn't locked the toes come up. The ball, instead of nosing over, falls groundward tailfirst. This can cost as much as ten yards in distance. Yale Lary of the Lions, one of the finest kickers of the 1960's, would say over and over to himself when he ran out on the field to kick, "Toes down, toes down, toes down."

The punted ball must rotate on its longitudinal axis; it must spiral. This gives distance to the kick and also aids in accuracy. It's the same as in passing. A quarterback would never throw an end-

The drop is the critical part of every punt. This is Steve O'Neal.

over-end pass to a receiver. He wants the ball to travel like a torpedo. You can usually tell a good punt by its sound. There's a deep thunk when the kicker's foot makes contact. A sharp thwack means good height but poor distance.

Most teams use a tight, balanced line when punting, often with a back stationed just forward of and on each side of the kicker. The linemen are instructed to protect to the inside, toward the center. There can't be, in the words of one coach, any "leaking at the seams."

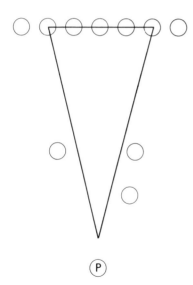

Blockers must keep clear a triangular area in front of the punter that looks like this.

The alignment is meant to keep clear a triangular zone just forward of the kicker. If an enemy player enters this area, it can result in a blocked kick. The base of the triangle extends from tackle to tackle. The kicker is at the triangle's apex. Backs are set to the right and left of the kicker to prevent the triangle from being penetrated from the sides.

The punter can't allow himself to be concerned by the pressure of the rush, nor can he permit the game situation to affect him. "The true test of any punter," says Jerrel Wilson, "is when it's late in the game and you're ahead but a field goal can beat you, and you have to go in and punt out of your own end zone.

"You know that you have to kick it far and high so it can't be returned. The pressure is really on. It's a situation that separates the men from the boys."

Once in a while the opposition players, by hurrying back to block for the return man, create an open field for the man doing the kicking. It's awfully inviting for the punter who likes to run with the ball. But any man who decides to turn ball carrier—without specific instructions from the coach—had better get yardage enough to make a first down. If he fails to do so, he would be wise to run someplace else besides his team's bench when he runs off the field after the play. It's not going to be very safe for him there.

Despite the presence
of Bill Peterson in
the "kicking zone,"
O'Neal gets his punt
away.

94

Occasionally a run from punt formation is pre-planned, with the kicker sweeping one of the ends behind a wall of blockers. About the only time you can expect to see a fake kick is when the kicking team has the ball on the opposition's side of the 50-yard line and thus can afford to gamble.

While Jerrel Wilson, in keeping with Hank Stram's wishes, has ranked as the most consistent punter in the American Football Conference, over in the National Conference, Bobby Joe Green has been wearing the laurels. Year in, year out, excellence has been the hallmark of his long career.

Even as a rookie Green impressed people. At the training camp of the Pittsburgh Steelers, Green's team in 1960 and 1961, he was nicknamed "The Rainmaker" because he boomed his kicks so high.

Born in Vernon, Texas, Green was five years old when he first began kicking the ball. As a high school player he displayed exceptional skill, once kicking from his own end zone to the opponent's 1-yard line, with the aid of good roll.

At the University of Florida, Green was a triple-threat halfback. Besides carrying the ball and passing it, he punted, place-kicked, and even drop-kicked a couple of times. He originally enrolled at the University of Oklahoma, where he was given instructions for improving his technique. But as his form grew more perfect, the distance of his kicks

Bobby Joe Green

dropped. After he transferred to Florida, he went back to kicking naturally and made speedy improvement. At 5-foot-11, 175, Green had a wiry build. When he was among his teammates, he looked smaller than he actually was because he wore no padding, just a helmet and shoulder pads.

When the Bears won the NFL championship in 1963, Green was their big offensive gun. When it came to running the ball and passing it, Chicago was less than formidable, but on almost any exchange of punts that season the Bears would pickup ten yards or so. Green averaged 46.5 yards per kick on 64 punts that season. His best year was 1961 when he averaged 47 yards per kick. A back injury threatened his career in 1968 but he made a successful comeback.

Green worked closely with the Bears' placekicker Mac Percival in team practice sessions, exchanging kicking tips. They watched each other in films and in games. "Bobby's been watching me long enough to know my correct pattern," said Percival. "When I deviate from it, I don't always know what the problem is, but he can tell."

In the latter stages of his career, Green was often asked the secret of his longevity. "Some punters last five years, some twenty years," he said. "It's more or less the condition you stay in." For Green, keeping in condition meant water-skiing during the off-season near his Gainesville, Florida, home. He

Dave Lewis unlimbers before a game.

credited the sport with relaxing him and keeping his back and legs strong.

Dave Lewis of the Cincinnati Bengals is another of the game's most noted punters. His 46.2-yard punting average in 1970 and his 44.8-yard average in 1971 were the highest in the NFL.

Lewis was a fine quarterback and standout college punter at Stanford, and then followed two seasons with Montreal in the Canadian Football League. In the fall of 1969, after flunking a tryout with the New York Giants, Lewis announced his retirement from pro football.

The following year, Bill Walsh, an assistant coach with the Bengals, contacted Lewis and convinced him to give pro football another try. Walsh had first seen Lewis play at Clovis High School in Clovis, California, and had coached him during his freshman year at Stanford.

Lewis impressed the coaches at the Cincinnati tryout camp early in 1970, and won a role as the team's No. 1 punter at training camp in July. He punted 79 times that season; not one kick was blocked and 43 weren't even returned. Bengal officials said that Lewis' punting was one of the chief factors that led to the team's winning of the Central Division championship of the American Football Conference.

Lewis employs a classic three-step style—with one difference. After getting the snap, he tends to hold the ball longer than other passers. The reason

Lewis holds the ball longer than most punters, but this time too long.

is to give his teammates time to get downfield. Lewis says that the Cincinnati center, Bob Johnson, snaps so quickly and so accurately that he can afford to hold the ball for the extra split second before kicking.

Dennis Partee of the San Diego Chargers and Don Cockroft of the Cleveland Browns are unusual among kickers because they do double duty; they both punt and place-kick. Coaches are constantly on the lookout for players with this skill because it gives them what amounts to another spot on the roster.

In days past, virtually all kickers played a twin role but doing so today is believed to be fraught with problems. Punting and place-kicking each require different skills, different sets of muscles. When a place-kicker tries to take on a punter's duties, his field-goal accuracy usually begins to suffer.

Or take what happened to Dennis Partee, who, after being drafted by the Chargers in 1968, immediately assumed the duties of both punter and place-kicker. Everything went along smoothly until 1970 when Partee began to experience pain whenever he tried to lock his ankle to place-kick. It hurt all the way up the front of his leg to the knee.

The Chargers told Partee to concentrate on punting exclusively and hired journeyman Mike Mercer to do the place-kicking. But the next season Partee experienced no pain and went back to handling both jobs. Again he was rated among the league's punting leaders and, with 87 points, one of the top scorers.

Partee did one thing differently when he reassumed his dual role. He began switching shoes to suit the kick, using a square-toe boot for place-kicking and one with a soft toe for punting.

You can talk about Partee's remarkable talent, and the punting superiority of Jerrel Wilson and

Dennis Partee of the Chargers is a double-duty kicker.

Don Cockroft keeps his punting shoe close by as he practices his place-kicking.

Bobby Joe Green, but their achievements pale when compared to those of one Clarence Herschberger, who played for the University of Chicago in the late 1890's. A 158-pound halfback who dropkicked, punted, and returned punts, Herschberger won distinction in 1898 as being the first non-Eastern player to be chosen for Walter Camp's All American team.

What is remarkable about Herschberger is that the punts that he returned were the ones that he kicked. In those days a team could, by recovering a punt of its own, win possession of the ball. Today, of course, the ball goes over to the receiving team, no matter which team makes the recovery.

Herschberger would sail the ball 40 or 50 yards downfield and then sprint after it, sometimes reaching it before his teammates or any of the opposition players. He once actually recovered one of his own kicks and sped into the end zone with it for a touchdown.

Football's hierarchy took a dim view of Herschberger's specialty, however. The fact that he was so successful with the play led to its being made illegal.

RETURNING KICKS

The Burlington Liars Club of Burlington, Wisconsin, annually attempts to find the world's greatest yarnspinner. In one recent year, the award went to a Racine man who told a story about a Green Bay football player "who ran back punts so fast that he often drew roughing-the-kicker penalties."

In another decade or so, if the present trend continues, the statement may not be so far-fetched, for running back punts, kickoffs, and missed place kicks is becoming more of an advanced art all the time. Coaches realize that a long runback is every bit as valuable as a completed pass or a recovered fumble, and often even more valuable.

Running back kicks was a haphazard business until fairly recent times. Coaches would spend every minute of every practice day rehearsing offensive and defensive plays and formations. Maybe they'd give fifteen minutes on Friday afternoon to "special teams," the term used to designate the squads that run back kicks, and those that seek to prevent them from being run back. But nowadays there's a coach in charge of special teams and at least one day a week is spent practicing the several plays his men use.

There are also strategy sessions involving special teams, with coaches reviewing films and scouting reports which reveal how their own and rival teams perform. It used to be, too, that coaches used rookie players or aging veterans—second-line players—on special teams. This practice is dying out. Coach Hank Stram says that his Kansas City Chiefs use their "best people" as special-team personnel. "We put athletes out there," says Stram, "men who can move and who can make the open-field block or tackle."

To be a member of a special team, a man has to be agile and have good speed, but mostly he has to be fearless. How fearless? Well, the injury rate for special-team personnel is about eight times what it is for any other position. That's why players refer to special teams as "suicide squads."

Speed is the reason for the suicidal nature of the job. On an ordinary run or pass play, most of the players move at a speed of about 7 miles an hour. But on a punt or kickoff, players fly, traveling at approximately 20 miles an hour for distances of 30 to 35 yards. When two players coming from opposite directions collide, something has to give. It's the chief reason why each team has a doctor sitting on the bench.

The man who does the returning of kicks has to be the most fearless of all. He has to be able to think clearly, despite the pressure, and act decisively. The men who return kickoffs are usually bigger and a bit stronger than the punt returners. They have more time to make the catch, tuck the ball away, and build up speed. Their size gives them the strength to be able to ward off the first hits

This page: Giants' kick returner Rocky Thompson is relaxed as he waits for the ball. After making the catch, he storms upfield.

Left: Returning kicks is a rugged job. Carl Garrett lies prone after being shaken up while carrying the ball on a kickoff.

The pressure of kick returning can trigger a disaster. Here the usually sure-handed Paul Robinson struggles.

and break early tackle attempts. Still, they have to have speed to be able to reach the opposition goal should the opportunity arise.

All return men have to have sure hands. In making the catch, the receiver positions himself so that he is beneath the ball as it comes down, his elbows braced at his sides. What he shouldn't do is reach out for the ball.

Equally important, he must keep his eyes on the ball until it is in his arms. "Look the ball into your hands," is how the coaches express it. Failure to do this leads to a bungled catch. It's not as easy as it sounds. As the receiver positions himself, he can hear the footsteps of enemy players bearing down on him and the sound of colliding bodies as his teammates block. But he mustn't take his eyes off the ball.

As the ball is kicked, the blocking forms. Five men up front comprise a forward wall. Behind this first line of defense, a four-man "wedge," which is meant to convoy the ball carrier upfield, takes shape. There is a close working relationship between the wedge and the return man.

The captain of the wedge watches the kick returner, and as soon as the man makes the catch, he yells for the wedge to take off. "If it's a good wedge," says Bob Gladieux, captain of special teams for the Patriots, "it's timed so that the runner is just three or four steps behind. If you get the wedge too far out in front, the opposition goes around you."

As the wedge wings upfield, the opposition players streak downfield. The resulting collision is pro football's most violent moment. Six members of the opposition are designated as "wedge busters," and it's their job to fling their bodies into the wedge and destroy it. This allows other players, called "headhunters," to attack the man with the ball.

As these paragraphs may imply, there is nothing fancy or complicated about kick return plays, and no great amount of technical knowledge is required. Kick returners, wedge members, wedge

Patriot wedgemen

busters, and headhunters have been described by one coach as "guys who don't know any better."

Actually, two men are set near the goal line as the kick returners. As one positions to make the catch, the other shouts instructions. Usually the direction in which the ball is kicked is what determines the route—right, left, or middle—that the return man will take. Sometimes, however, he follows a predetermined strategy. Teams study films of opponents' games, looking for weak spots. They might detect a player who takes it easy going downfield, or maybe a rookie who is so eager to

On a sideline return, blockers race across the field in an attempt to set up a protected corridor for the return man (R), who is convoyed by his four-man wedge. At the same time, opposition players careen downfield.

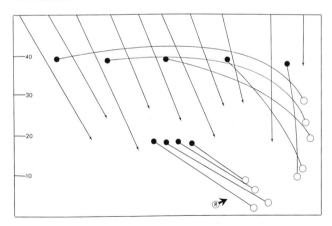

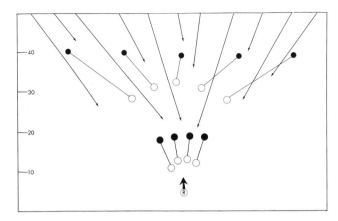

Here the return man heads straight up the middle. Blockers drop back to form what amounts to a pair of wedges.

display his talents that he outraces his teammates, leaving his lane unprotected. The return man will be instructed to target his run at the vulnerable point.

When a team employs an up-the-middle return, it usually features cross-blocking, that is, the blockers on each side of the return path cross from one side to another as they charge upfield, the idea being to slam the opposition players to the outside, creating clear passage for the ball carrier.

While kickoff return plays may be said to lack in finesse, they are somewhat more sophisticated than those of an earlier time. In 1933 the Boston Redskins hired William (Lone Star) Dietz as head coach, a man who loved trick plays. One of his favorites involved kickoff returns. When the Redskins received a kickoff, the team would huddle at about the 10-yard line, and the man who made the catch would hand the ball to someone else. Then, on a signal, the whole team would suddenly disperse, each man going in a different direction. It wasn't very artful but it worked and sometimes runbacks of 40 or 50 yards were the result. The play was aptly named. It was called "the squirrel cage."

Before he retired in 1972, Gale Sayers of the Chicago Bears was the game's most devastating kick returner. Sayers had good speed and he could accelerate quickly, but his moves were his chief talent. He could cut and fake instinctively, changing direction in the blink of an eye, going left or right, wherever there appeared the smallest glimmer of daylight.

Sayers wasted no time establishing his eminence. He was the NFL's Rookie of the Year in 1965, a season in which he averaged 31.4 yards per kickoff return. Teams kicking off to the Bears often kicked short so that Sayers couldn't get his hands on the ball. Giving Chicago good field position, they reasoned, was better than letting Sayers try for six points.

Some coaches would instruct their kickers to boot the ball deep but angle it away from Sayers. So Gale took to lining up under the goal post with his return partner. As the ball was kicked, Sayers would yell "Right!" or "Left!"—indicating the side of the field the other man was to cover. Sayers would then race to make the catch. Six times in his career Sayers ran back kickoffs for touchdowns, a record which he shared with Ollie Matson. The record has since been equalled by Travis Williams.

One return of Sayers stands out in his mind. It took place in 1965, his rookie season, and resulted in one of the 22 touchdowns he scored that year. Two minutes were left in the game when the Minnesota Vikings scored to take a 6-point lead. The Viking players were congratulating one another on the sidelines when the referee's whistle signaled the kickoff.

Sayers gathered in the ball and roared straight up the middle behind his wedge. As the blocking began to collapse, Sayers veered to his left as a would-be tackler hurtled past, cut to his right at the 40-yard line to avoid another man, then spurted into the end zone. He had gone 97 yards without a hand touching him.

Travis Williams of the Los Angeles Rams, known as "The Road Runner," inherited Sayers' mantle as the game's foremost kick returner. A rare combination of power and blinding speed, Williams led all NFL return men in 1971 with a 29.7-yard average. But earlier in his career he did even better. In 1967 he established a record of 41.1 yards per return. Coaches then began in-

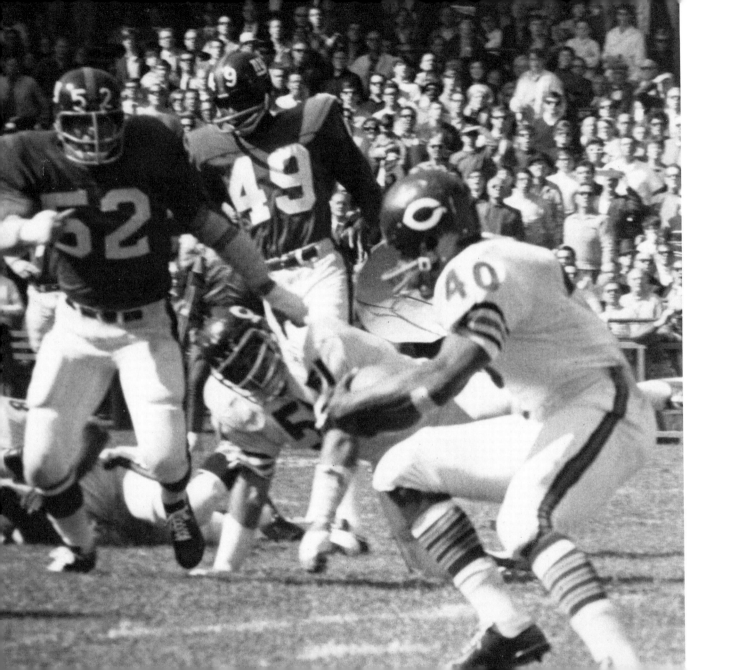

structing their kickers to kick the ball anywhere as long as it didn't go to Williams.

The strategy doesn't always work. In a game against the Pittsburgh Steelers, Chuck Noll, the Steeler coach, told his kicker not to kick into the end zone to Williams. He didn't want him to be able to build up momentum for a long run. "Keep it short," Noll ordered. The kick went high and shallow. Williams darted forward and was there when the ball came down. His wedge was there, too. Someone yelled "Go!" and Williams went— 96 yards for a touchdown.

Williams, who spent four seasons with the Green Bay Packers before being traded to the Rams, didn't always operate so effectively. Returning a kick in 1967, his rookie year, he turned on an extra burst of speed and ran into his wedge, knocking himself unconscious. He also went through a period when he couldn't seem to stop fumbling. To express the team's sentiment, one of the Packers taped a suitcase handle to a football and left it in Williams' locker.

Williams has bullet speed. He's been timed at 9.3 seconds for 100 yards. He sped for four touchdowns on kickoff returns during his rookie year, and no one, rookie or veteran, had ever done that

Right: **Travis Williams, "The Road Runner"**

109

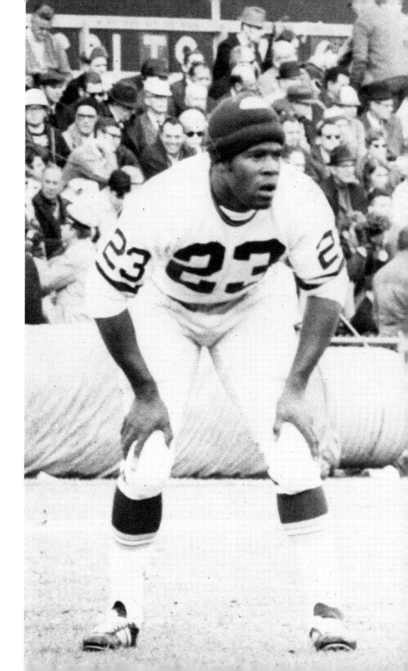

Giants' kick coverage brings six tacklers veering in on Cliff Harris of the Dallas Cowboys.

before. He added a fifth touchdown in 1969, and the sixth in 1971.

All pro teams follow pretty much the same strategy in seeking to thwart players like Williams. Members of the kickoff team race downfield abreast, spacing themselves in running lanes. As they approach the ball carrier, they veer toward him. The closing-in point is determined by the length of the kick and the man who's running it back. When Gale Sayers was in his prime, the opposition closed in very quickly.

It used to be that coverage teams were made up of big, strong men, but more and more, agility is becoming a factor. These men have to be able to avoid being blocked, and size and strength do not necessarily help in this regard.

The two outside men are usually the fastest of all. Their role is critical. They must get downfield before anyone else, so as to shut off the corridor along the sidelines. Should the ball carrier be able to get outside these men, he's almost certain to get good distance. The two men on either side of the kicker have to be speedsters, too. It's their responsibility to prevent the runback man from building up momentum through the middle. All members of the coverage team have to be reliable tacklers. A miss can be disasterous.

As for the kicker, after he's put the ball into the air, followed through, and regained his balance, he angles to the ball carrier's side of the field, serving as a safety, the last line of defense. He is less than perfect in this regard. Most kickers are prepared neither physically or mentally for tackling, and they pursue the man with the ball with about the same enthusiasm a schoolboy displays on returning to the classroom in the fall.

Returning kickoffs is not the same as returning punts. For one thing, it's not quite so hazardous. Indeed, the single most perilous job in pro football is that of punt returner.

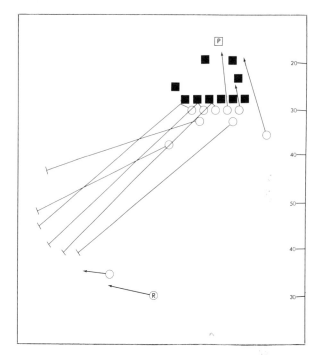

Most teams try to return punts along one sideline. Linemen drop off to give blocking support.

Because he's concentrating on the ball, the punt returner never really knows how close the opposition is. And there's no protective wedge when he fields punts. One man, or perhaps two, may get back, but seldom more than two. It usually is the fate of the punt returner to be gang-tackled in the open field.

Very few coaches allow their running stars to run back punts. Gale Sayers did, but only as a rookie. O. J. Simpson of the Buffalo Bills never has. An exception to the rule is Leroy Kelly of the Cleveland Browns, one of the successful running backs *and* punt returners of recent times.

Kelly, once he has the ball in his possession, rockets away. He accelerates so quickly that he often goes by men who are poised to tackle him. In the open, he uses his speed with finesse. He'll burst through a hole, then come to almost a complete stop for a split second as he sizes up the defense, deciding in which direction he should zoom to pick up the most yardage. He's a master at following a blocker, staying with the man until he comes under attack, then swerving away.

Long runbacks on punt returns are rare and touchdowns hardly ever happen. Leroy Kelly averaged 9.7 yards per return in 1971, which was tops in the American Football Conference. The No. 1 kickoff return man in pro football that year, Travis Williams, averaged more than three times that much on his returns—29.7 yards.

Punt returners used to achieve a great deal more yardage than they do nowadays, twice as much, in fact. In 1941, the Chicago Bears led the league in kick returning with an average of 20.2 yards per return. In 1948, the Bears averaged 19.1 yards per return. But in 1972, the Miami Dolphins, who topped the league in punt returning, averaged only

Leroy Kelly

10.5 yards per return.

It's not that players today are less skilled or more cowardly. There was a tactical change, one that is usually credited to Paul Brown, recognized as one

112

of pro football's most astute innovators.

During the late 1940's and early 1950's, when Brown coached the Cleveland Browns, the team boasted the game's best punter in Horace Gillom. It was then usual for the punter to line up nine or ten yards behind the line of scrimmage, but Brown instructed Gillom to go back fifteen yards. Gillom's kicks were so long that the extra distance he went back hardly mattered.

By standing back fifteen yards, Gillom didn't need a great deal of blocking protection. He was able to get his kick away before anyone was upon him. The men in the line merely had to brush block, and then could race downfield to prevent a

As Tom Blanchard punts, his Giant teammates head downfield to stop the runback.

"Fair catch," signals Rick Volk.

runback. So many of them got downfield so quickly that they usually flattened the return man right after he made the catch or just as he was making it. Shorter runbacks—and braver return men—were the result.

The widespread use of the fair catch also dates to this period. A fair catch is one that's made after the return man has signaled, by means of an upraised hand, that he will not run with the ball. He therefore may not be tackled. For the ensuing down, the ball is placed down at the point of the catch. A return man will call for a fair catch when the opposition is bearing down on him and he realizes that no significant return is possible.

Coaches recognize the fair catch for what it is—a "nothing" play. There's no forward progress. It can even be detrimental, for if the receiver muffs the catch the ball becomes free. About the only beneficial feature of the fair catch, as opposed to a ball that's run back, is that it stops the clock. You see more fair catches in the closing minutes of a half than at any other time during the game.

Some players disdain the fair catch and will attempt a runback even when they know that a horde of enemy players is thundering toward them. Ron Smith, punt returner for the Chicago Bears, is one such player. Some of his teammates have told him that he is tempting fate by attempting to run back every punt, but he shrugs off their warnings.

"If I was afraid," he says, "I wouldn't be helping the team. I don't believe there's a man in this league big enough to tear me apart. And when I get a step or two, the combination of my weight and speed equalizes things against those 260-pounders."

Most teams station their fastest player as their deepest return man, and station a second return man about ten yards in front of him to handle short punts. The deep man takes his position approximately ten yards deeper than the punter's average kick. For instance, if the punter is known to average 40 yards per kick, as measured from the line of scrimmage, the deep man drops back 50 yards from the line of scrimmage. The short man goes back 40 yards.

The two men work as a team, shouting instructions to one another. If it's a short kick and the opposition is pounding downfield, the deep man will instruct the short man to make a fair catch. Or if the short man has a chance to make a return, the deep man will run up and block. When the deep man makes the catch, the short man blocks.

Meanwhile, the linemen, after either rushing the kicker or blocking in the line, wheel around and race downfield to aid the return man by setting up a "wall" close to one of the sidelines. Sometimes it's called a "picket line." It's been designated in advance whether the return is to go to the right or left. Occasionally it goes up the center.

The return man is likely to first head up the middle of the field, hoping to draw the opposition players there, and he then cuts to the side where the wall has been set up. It's a wild footrace to outdistance the tacklers and get behind the wall. Once there, he sprints along the sideline for as long as the wall holds fast. If he sees a breakdown ahead, he cuts back toward the middle.

Teams don't always concentrate on running back punts in the manner described above. The game situation may dictate other strategy. For example, a team may make a strong rush in attempting to block a punt and gain possession of the ball. Just about every player will be sent blazing in. The return men are told of this strategy and may be instructed, since they aren't going to have any blockers, to fair-catch the ball.

Each man on the team doing the punting has a clearcut responsibility in defending against the return. If one or two men should fail to carry out their assignments, it can lead to a long runback, even a touchdown.

The ends, since their role isn't critical in protecting the punter, are the first to race downfield. They try to force the play to the inside. The backs often cover outside the ends.

Of course, the best defense against a long runback is a ball that stays aloft five seconds. For the men on the punting team, happiness is a ball that hangs.

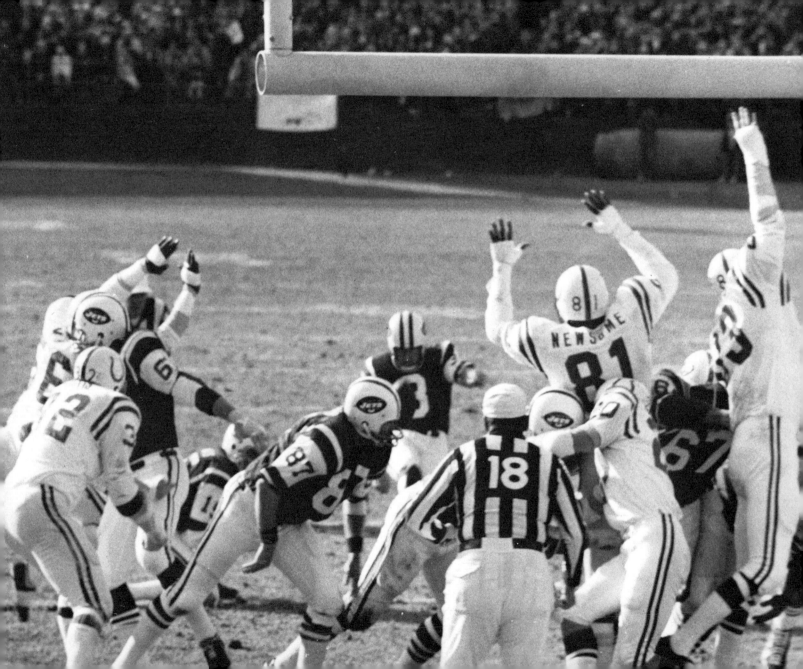

BLOCKING KICKS

Anytime a team can block a kick of any type—a punt, an extra-point attempt, or a field-goal attempt—it's a big play. It can turn a game around.

But it doesn't happen very often. The Baltimore Colts have established themselves as one of pro football's most successful teams when it comes to blocking kicks. During one recent season, Colt defenders managed to block seven field-goal tries, three punts, and one extra-point try—eleven kicks in all.

Two reasons why the Colts stood out in this department were linebacker Ted Hendricks and defensive end Bubba Smith. Both were 6-foot-7, agile, and strong. The Colts would use either to "shoot the gap," to burst through an opening in the line. Bubba went first. If he couldn't get through, the Colts would then shoot Hendricks. If both Smith and Hendricks were stopped, Jerry Logan, a safety, would bolt into whatever gap he might spot.

During a game at Shea Stadium in 1971, Hendricks leaped high to get a hand in front of a PAT attempt off the instep of Bobby Howfield of the Jets. The ball never reached the crossbar and the

Leaping high, his right hand almost touching the crossbar, the Colt's Ted Hendricks (83, far right) managed to block this point-after attempt by Bobby Howfield of the Jets.

117

Colts went on to win, 14-13. Jet Coach Weeb Ewbank, after reviewing films of the game, said, "Our defense broke down and Hendricks got across the line. Nobody ever should."

To get a man across the line—that's the basic goal of teams attempting to block a field goal or point-after try. The defense first tries to force an opening, then sends a man careening through. It's seldom that a player streaming in from the outside can get to the ball in time.

To create the opening in the line, teams vary players' blocking assignments. Here's one example:

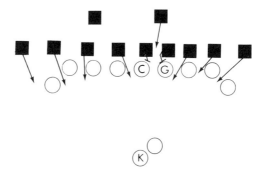

The player in the middle of the line hits into the right shoulder of the offensive center (C) so as to drive him to the left. The tackle charges into the left shoulder of the guard (G) opposite him, nudging the man to the right. The safety then pours through the gap.

Giants' Pete Athas builds a high "wall."

Of course, other members of the defensive team are charging, too. Eight men are usually employed to rush on a field-goal attempt. The other three keep alert for a fake kick and the ensuing run or pass. It looks like this:

Sometimes nine men rush:

It used to be common practice for a small man, if he wasn't able to penetrate, to vault onto the shoulders of his bigger teammates. With his hands upstretched, he presented a "wall" that was eleven or twelve feet in height. But this practice was outlawed early in 1973. It's now illegal for a player to jump on, or stand on, or be picked up by a teammate in an effort to block a kick.

There's always a great deal of "stunting" in the line. Players abruptly switch and alter their positions just before the ball is snapped, in an effort to confuse the opposition.

When a team attempts a long-distance field goal against the Kansas City Chiefs, the Chiefs sometimes set up an unusual defense in the person of Morris Stroud, at 6-foot-10, the tallest player in

New York Giants try in vain to stop a field-goal attempt by Jim O'Brien of the Colts.

pro football. Stroud positions himself right in front of the goal posts. As the ball gets near, Stroud jumps up like a center in basketball, and tries to deflect it away from the crossbar. He's a one-man team.

There's shouting in the line, too, plenty of it. Quarterback Earl Morrall, who held the ball for Jim O'Brien when he booted the game-winning field goal against the Dallas Cowboys in Super Bowl V, remembers the last frantic seconds before the kick. "The Cowboys yelled and screamed at O'Brien as he lined up," says Morrall. " 'He's going to miss!,' one guy shouted. 'He's going to choke!' I heard another scream.

"Then they called a timeout, and they didn't have any timeouts left. They just were doing everything they could think of to rattle poor O'Brien. But he didn't rattle."

When attempting to block a punt, defensive tactics are somewhat different. Sometimes the rushmen will go all out in their attempt to block, but other times the effort will be halfhearted, with the defense concentrating on the runback instead. It depends on the game situation—the score, the time remaining, the team's field position, and so on. It also depends on how efficiently the punting team is known to perform.

If the kicker is known to be slow—that is, if it takes him more than 2.3 seconds to get the ball into the air—he's likely to experience many zealous rushes. The same holds true if the defense finds a weakness in the line and believes it can shoot a man through. A center who is slow or inaccurate with his snaps can be another reason a team rushes all out.

If the game situation is such that the opposition *must* have the ball, they'll rush—naturally. The obvious example is when a team is trailing in the closing minutes of a game.

Anytime a punter must kick from deep within his own territory, from inside the 10-yard line, say, he can expect the opposition to come piling in. They realize that a kick that is blocked and recovered can possibly reap a touchdown.

Bobby Joe Green of the Chicago Bears, who had only three punts blocked in an NFL career that spanned more than a decade, expressed the attitude that most punters have toward blocked kicks when he said, "You can't get gun-shy and worry about things like that. There's nothing you can do. You've got to have a certain type of temperament to be a punter anyway. You've got to be able to go along with the tide."

The usual method of attempting to block a punt is to overload one side of the line. For instance, two fast linebackers (L) will blaze in from the same side as the ball is snapped, the hope being that only one of them will be blocked:

His punt attempt blocked by the Jets' John Ebersole, Jim McCann of the 49ers sets out in pursuit of the ball.

Or two members of the defensive line, often a tackle and an end, will attack together. Usually the back (B) on the kicker's off side is their target. The idea is for one of the men to draw the back out of position, which may leave a clear path to the kicker. It looks like this:

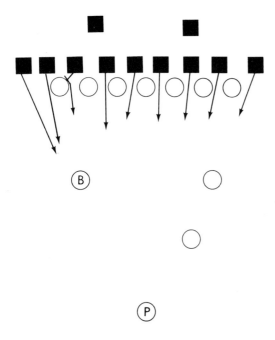

Other times the charge goes up the middle. In this example, cross-blocking is meant to create a gap for the safety to sluice through:

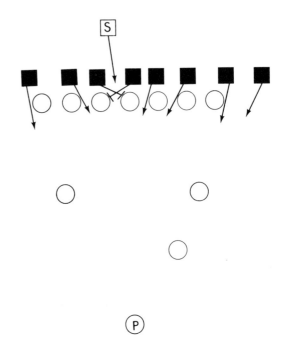

Players seeking to block punts look for the tiniest clue that might tip off when the ball is going to be snapped. In a recent game between the Giants and the Eagles, the Eagles noticed that the Giant center would tilt the ball slightly just before he snapped it back. So they began timing their charges, not with the snap, but with the tilt. The rushmen deflected one punt and wrecked another by tackling the New York punter just as he caught the ball.

It takes courage to block a punt. The rushmen have to leap high, their arms upraised, aiming for a spot about two yards in front of the kicker's kicking foot. "You've got to stick your face right in there in order to be able to do any good," says one player. If the rushmen fail to block, they must recover, turn, and then race in the opposite direction to protect the return man.

It would probably be more efficient if the rushmen directed their attack at the kicker himself, instead of at a spot in front of the man, but striking the kicker can lead to a roughing-the-kicker penalty. This costs the guilty team fifteen yards; in addition, the punting team is granted a first down.

"Avoiding the kicker," says the rulebook, "is the primary responsibility of defensive players . . ." This doesn't mean that rushmen are always punished when contact is made. It's up to the referee to decide. If a rushman who blocks a kick charges so violently that his momentum carries him into the kicker, it's judged an "incidental part of a successful play." No penalty is assessed. But there's a penalty if the rushman merely brushes the kicker.

Punters frequently resort to fakery in an effort to influence the referee's decision. A rushman will accidentally graze the kicker's leg or side, and suddenly the man will topple to the ground as if poleaxed. Sometimes it works; usually it doesn't.

Cleveland's Gary Collins, the NFL's No. 1

punter in 1965, was a master at earning roughing-the-kicking penalties for his team. When an opposing player happened to touch him, no matter how tentatively, Collins would recoil as if struck by an express bus, and then plop to the ground where he would writhe pathetically. The performance became known as the "Gary Collins Swan Dive."

Giants' Tom Blanchard gets his punt away despite John Ward's desperate leap.

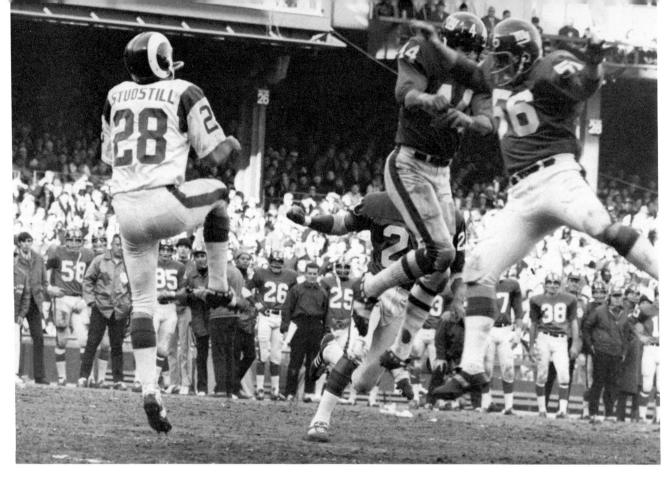

Tom Longo (44) and Pat Hughes (56) of the New York Giants converge in midair in an unsuccessful try to bat down Pat Studstill's punt.

Larry Seiple of the Miami Dolphins was another punter with a theatrical bent. One year in a game against the Buffalo Bills, the Bills were penalized twice for roughing Seiple. "They ought to nominate me for an Oscar," said Seiple after the game. "I thought I did a great acting job."

QUICK KICKS, SQUIBS, AND OTHER STRATEGY

John (Paddy) Driscoll, who played for the Chicago Cardinals and later the Bears during the 1920's, while most noted as a drop-kicker, was also a fine punter. Driscoll didn't achieve great distance with his kicks but he was extremely skilled in placing them.

On Thanksgiving Day, 1925, the Cards, Driscoll's team at the time, faced the Bears in a game that marked the debut of the great Red Grange. As a professional, Grange's sensational running at Illinois had earned him the nickname of "The Galloping Ghost" and recognition as the outstanding college football star of the 1920's, the "Golden Era" of sport, as it's been called. More than 36,000 fans, the largest crowd in pro football history, packed Wrigley Field in anticipation of seeing Grange run wild.

But Grange did nothing that day. Driscoll's punting was the reason. He booted 23 punts and all but three times managed to angle the ball away from Grange. The game ended in a scoreless tie.

As the players were leaving the field, several thousand fans booed loudly. "What a shame to hear the fans boo Red Grange," Driscoll said to his wife as they were driving home. "He's a nice young fella!"

125

"Don't feel sorry for *him*," she said. "They were booing *you*."

Alas, kickers with Driscoll's remarkable skill at placing the ball have gone the way of the cloche helmet and the two-legged goal post. The idea today is to simply boom the ball straight downfield.

To be able to earn your keep as a punter in days gone by, you had to be able to execute "coffin-corner" kicks. The coffin corners were those two corners of the field that included the defending team's goal line, and that portion of either sideline

Paddy Driscoll (center) poses with two of Chicago's backfield men of the 1940's, Bill Osmanski (left) and George McAfee.

within ten yards of the goal. A punter would deliberately punt out of bounds in this area, putting the receiving team desperately close to its own end zone on ensuing play from scrimmage.

College punters occasionally use coffin-corner strategy, but in the pro game it's as rare as the jump pass. The reason has to do with a punter's ability to be consistent, the one vital characteristic each must have. Kicking to the coffin corner usually involves letting up on the kick and this wrecks consistency. Coaches would rather see their punters thunder the ball beyond the goal line, even though it results in a touchback, meaning that the opposition gets possession on the 20-yard line.

Punter Jerrel Wilson of the Chiefs explains it this way: "To be consistent, you have to be in the groove. If you vary from that groove, you risk losing consistency.

"I'm an 'attack' punter. Every time I kick, I try to get the ball as far and as high as I can. I could never kick it any other way."

Other kickers claim that trying to punt out of bounds is asking for trouble. "There's too much chance of having the ball slide off your foot," says one. "By trying for a sideline, you can wind up with a nice 9-yarder."

During the mid-1960's, the Detroit Lions employed a novel kicking play, a cousin to the coffin-corner kick. Detroit's punter at the time was Yale Lary, a superb kicker who led the league in punting three times, in 1959, 1961, and 1963. But the play didn't involve Lary. It was executed by Earl Morrall, the team's quarterback and No. 2 punter. Morrall wasn't able to get the distance Lary could with his kicks, and that was what made him valuable. He was the Lions' "short kicker."

If Detroit was forced into a punting situation with the ball on the opposition's 45-yard line, say, Morrall would kick. No use having Lary come in. He was so strong that he would rocket the ball into the end zone and the opposition would have a first down on their 20-yard line. This didn't happen when Earl booted. Even when he kicked with all his power, the ball would seldom go more than 35 or 40 yards. "It was a terrific play," Morrall recalls. "Quite a few times the ball stopped dead inside the opposition's 5-yard line. What could be better than that?"

Punters of the past also had to know how to execute the quick kick, another piece of strategy that's no longer seen, at least in professional football. A better name for the quick kick might be "surprise punt." It was a punt that was booted on second or third down, when the opposition safety man was playing up close to the line of scrimmage.

It was a potent weapon. Since there was no man deep to receive the punt, there was little likelihood of a runback. A kick with good roll often resulted in a gain of 50 or 60 yards.

In order to work, the quick kick has to evolve

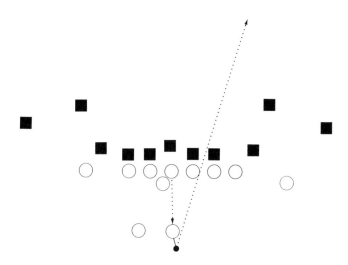

In the quick kick from the T formation, the quarterback slides to one side, allowing the snap to go directly to deep back. The idea is to soar the ball behind the safeties.

from what looks like a conventional running or passing play, with the man who is to do the kicking positioned as one of the running backs (see diagram). As the quarterback calls the signals, the man who is to do the kicking backs up two steps. At the same time the quarterback slides to one side, allowing the center to snap the ball all the way back. There's not sufficient time for a conventional three-step approach. One step has to do; it's simply step and kick.

The quick kick was one of Sammy Baugh's favorite weapons. It was relatively easy to execute from the single-wing formation, which the Redskins used, because the tailback received a direct pass from center, the way the punter does today.

Baugh used the quick kick with devastating effect in the Redskins-Bears meeting for the NFL championship in 1942. The opening kickoff went to the Redskins and their return man was flattened on the Washington 12-yard line. Baugh's reputation as a passer was already well established and the Bear defense expected him to come out throwing. Sam took the snap from center, cocked his arm and drifted back. "Pass! Pass!" he heard the Chicago defenders shout.

Then suddenly Baugh lowered the ball, held it in both hands, and without breaking stride swung his foot into it, sending a low line drive over the head of the safetyman. The ball struck down at midfield, bounced forward and kept rolling and rolling. It stopped at the Chicago 5-yard line. By the time the Bears recovered from the shock, the Redskins had the game well in hand.

The quick kick is still used in college play. Some quick-kickers use the "rocker" technique, which involves rocking on the right foot while stepping backward and then forward on the left, then kicking with the right foot. Other quick-kick specialists use the "runback" method. After receiving the ball, they quickly back up three steps—right, left, right.

Sammy Baugh, master of the quick kick

They then step forward with the left foot, then kick.

The reason that the quick kick has gone out of style in pro football is that there are no more

Sammy Baughs, no players who are multitalented. Backfield men today are specialists, able to run, pass, or receive passes. There are no punters back there, at least not until a punting situation arrives. This, plus the fact that teams today have no wish to give up the ball on third down, has shunted the quick kick into oblivion. Why punt, coaches reason, when you've got a Jan Stenerud or Tom Dempsey who can get you three points from 50 yards away?

But some day the quick kick may be revived. "Sometimes these things have a way of coming back," says Hank Stram. "You never know. We're getting good college coaches into the game, and you may begin to see things like the coffin-corner kick and the quick kick."

The option of varying kicks doesn't belong to punters exclusively. Place-kickers, when they're kicking off, have a number of subtle pieces of strategy that they can attempt. The best known is the onside kick. (Actually, anytime the entire team is behind the ball when it is being kicked, it is an onside kick. But in recent years, the term has come to refer only to the particular type of kick described below.)

In executing an onside kick, the kicker approaches the ball just as if it were a conventional kickoff, but instead of exploding the ball far downfield, he kicks a low rifle shot which travels the minimum of ten yards, then, hopefully, caroms off

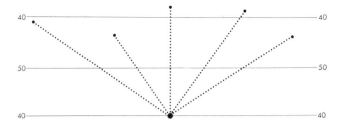

An onside kick is directed to any one of several pre-planned points.

an opposition player toward a teammate who is trying to recover it. Teams use the onside kick when possession of the ball is vital.

The ball is never kicked haphazardly. It's aimed at any one of several prearranged spots (see diagram).

Another kick that place-kickers occasionally use when kicking off is the squib kick. The word "squib," according to the dictionary, means a firecracker that burns but does not explode, and that pretty much defines a squib kick. It's a kick that fizzles.

The ball is placed on its side, the tip angled slightly to the left or right, and it is kicked full force from that position. The result is a short kick that bounces crazily. Members of the receiving team usually try to smother it as if it were a fumble. There's seldom any runback.

Jim Turner, once the kicker for the New York Jets, had trouble sending his kickoffs deep enough during 1970. Of the 45 he attempted, 39 were returned, and O. J. Simpson of the Buffalo Bills and Homer Jones of the Cleveland Browns ran back kickoffs for touchdowns. In an effort to prevent long runbacks, Jet coach Weeb Ewbank ordered Turner to squib his kickoffs. No kicker likes to be told to squib the ball. It's something like a manager telling a homerun hitter to bunt. Turner was embarrassed by the policy.

There are other variations of the kickoff. For example, Jan Stenerud of the Chiefs can execute a kickoff kick while pretending to place the ball on the tee. But such departures from the norm are rarely seen. What coaches want on kickoffs are deep kicks, ones that go beyond the end line, and that's the type that place-kickers practice.

No book about kicking would be complete without mention of the drop kick. Used much as a place kick is today (except when kicking off), the drop kick was at one time as much a part of the game as chalk stripes and cleated shoes. Its name describes it; it was executed by dropping the ball and kicking it as it rebounded.

The ball was held in both hands and tilted back slightly, then dropped from just above knee level. As he dropped, the kicker stepped forward with his left foot, gathering power, then swung his right foot into the ball. It took perfect timing.

As a Jet, Jim Turner was made to squib the ball.

The kicker's stance varied somewhat, depending on the distance of the kick. On an extra-point try, or any short kick, the kicker crouched as he took his stance, which enabled him to lean into the ball and reduce the distance of the drop. Both of these features aided accuracy.

On a longer kick attempt, the kicker stood more erect. Only in this way could he get a full leg swing necessary to send the ball over the longer distance.

Most drop-kickers made contact with the toes of the right foot. But the kick could also be executed with the instep. In such cases, the ball was dropped at more of an angle so that, following the rebound, it would be positioned lengthwise on the instep as the leg swung through, much as in a conventional punt.

Just as no two place-kickers of the present day kick the ball in exactly the same way, so, too, there were many styles of drop-kicking. Alexander Moffat of Princeton, who drop-kicked four field goals in the first half of a game against Harvard in 1883, angled the ball toward him as he prepared to drop, varying the angle with the distance of the kick. The greater the distance, the wider the angle. A journalist of the day praised Moffat's style as being "sure and quick." Other players held the ball so that it pointed away from them, toward the goal.

Walter Camp, often called "the father of American football" and a prominent figure in the sport for almost half a century, played halfback at Yale

The Moffat style of drop-kicking

The Camp style

131

and also drop-kicked. He had an unusual style, holding one end of the ball in the palm of his right hand. To drop the ball, he allowed it to nose over and strike down on the other end, whereupon he swung his right foot through, aiming the toes at a point directly below the laces.

Blocking in the line was not done with nearly the efficiency it is today, and thus drop-kickers of the 1880's had to have the ability to dodge onrushing opponents before kicking. Many kickers of the day learned to drop-kick with either foot. *St. Nicholas* magazine, self-described as "an illustrated magazine for young folks," explained why: "For example, a right tackle breaks through and makes directly for the kick. In this case, the use of the right foot enables a man to kick without moving from his position . . . but in the use of the left foot, there is a possibility of kicking directly into the tackle. Thus a man who could use only his left foot would be forced to dodge the tackle first, and lose the accuracy of his aim . . ."

The longest drop kick of football's early days was the work of dark-haired, firm-jawed Pat O'Dea, an Australian who attended the University of Wisconsin. O'Dea's kick, with Northwestern the victim, traveled 62 yards, only one yard less than the present-day pro record for a *place*-kicked field goal.

The game was played in a swirling snowstorm, and when O'Dea lined up to kick he could barely see the goal posts because of the gloom and falling snow. The ball soared high above the players, then seemed to settle as it neared the goal, but the wind happened to be at O'Dea's back and a gust carried the ball the rest of the way. It grazed the crossbar as it went over. O'Dea was so much of a specialist that a contemporary once referred to him as being "practically useless for anything but kicking."

The great Jim Thorpe was hailed for his skill as a drop-kicker. In 1923, when Thorpe was a member of the Toledo Maroons, the team faced the Kansas City Cowboys in an exhibition game, played on a rain-soaked field. Thorpe kicked the ball between the uprights to give the Maroons a 3-0 victory. It traveled 40 yards.

Steve Owen, one of the Cowboy players and later to be coach of the New York Giants, protested the kick, saying that Thorpe had punted the ball. "Nobody could drop-kick a spiral forty yards in the mud," Owen declared.

But later Owen changed his mind. "Maybe he did drop-kick that ball forty yards in the mud," said Owen. "He could do nearly everything else."

The era of the drop kick began to fade during the 1920's. As the ball lost its overall roundness, its pudginess, kickers had difficulty getting a true bounce. Then the rules were changed to prohibit a running kick. With the kicker stationary, there was no reason not to have a holder. Thus, the place kick became pre-eminent.

Jim Thorpe drop-kicks.

During the 1940's, the drop kick could still be seen occasionally. But when Lou Groza and Ben Agajanian began demonstrating their enormous place-kicking skill, the drop kick all but disappeared.

Some experts say that drop-kicking could play a meaningful role in modern football, that the drop kick is as reliable as the place kick. They point to modern rugby in which the *running* drop kick is still an integral part of the game. If a rugby player can drop-kick a ball while speeding downfield, they argue, then a football player should be able to drop-kick from a standing-still position.

"You can drop-kick a football just as easily as you can place-kick it accurately," says Dr. Edward J. Storey in his book, *Secrets of Kicking the Football.* "Today's football is easier to slice or hook than was the old wide pre-1934 ball, but the problem is no greater in the drop kick than it is in the place kick. The modern ball is also lighter than the old-fashioned model, and this difference is an advantage for today's kicker."

One obvious advantage of the drop kick is that it releases the man who would ordinarily hold the ball for blocking duty. It's also regarded as superior in the event of a poor pass from center. In the frantic moments that follow, the drop-kicker, after recovering the ball, can kick on the run. The place-kicker can only run.

Some kickers of the present-day occasionally

tinker with the drop kick during practice sessions. Tom Dempsey of the Eagles is highly skilled in the art. "I wouldn't be afraid to try a drop kick on an extra-point attempt," says Dempsey. "I'd even try one in a tie game."

Getting a coach to agree to go along with the idea is another matter. Virtually all coaches feel that there is too much risk involved. "The fact that the ball must bounce introduces a greater possibility of error," says Pete Retzlaff, general manager of the Philadelphia Eagles. "And everything we do is designed to eliminate errors."

However, the problem of bounce isn't as acute as it used to be. Artificial surfaces, like AstroTurf, which are now in widespread use, contain no bumps or divots, no hard spots or soft spots. The kicker is sure of getting a perfect bounce. But the other problem—the streamlined ball—remains. There is no likelihood that the football will ever go back to the pumpkin ball.

If you should ever happen to see a drop kick in a game, it's likely to occur on an extra-point attempt. The holder will muff the center's snap. The kicker will pick up the ball and scamper to one side to elude the onrushing linemen. Suddenly he'll stop, drop the ball, and quickly boot it through the uprights for the point.

Some day it's going to happen.

ALL-TIME SCORING RECORDS

Total Points
1,742—George Blanda, Oakland Raiders
1,608—Lou Groza, Cleveland Browns
1,130—Gino Cappelletti, New England Patriots

ALL-TIME PLACE-KICKING RECORDS

Points After Touchdown

Most Seasons Leading League
6—George Blanda, Oakland Raiders

Most Points After Touchdown, Lifetime
824—George Blanda, Oakland Raiders

Most Points After Touchdown, Season
64—George Blanda, Oakland Raiders (Houston Oilers, 1961)

Most Points After Touchdown, Game
9—Pat Harder, Chicago Cardinals vs. New York Giants, October 17, 1948

Most Consecutive Points After Touchdown
245—George Blanda, Oakland Raiders, 1967–1972

Field Goals

Most Seasons Leading League
5—Lou Groza, Cleveland Browns

Most Field Goals, Lifetime
288—George Blanda, Oakland Raiders

Most Field Goals, Season
34—Jim Turner, Denver Broncos (New York Jets, 1968)

Most Field Goals, Game
7—Jim Bakken, St. Louis Cardinals vs. Pittsburgh Steelers, September 24, 1967.

Most Consecutive Field Goals
16—Jan Stenerud, Kansas City Chiefs, 1969

Longest Field Goal
63 yards—Tom Dempsey, New Orleans Saints vs. Detroit Lions, November 8, 1970

ALL-TIME PUNTING RECORDS

Most Seasons Leading League
4—Sammy Baugh, Washington Redskins

Most Punts, Lifetime
888—Bobby Joe Green, Chicago Bears

Longest Punt
98 yards—Steve O'Neal, New York Jets vs. Denver Broncos, September 21, 1969

Highest Average, Lifetime
45.1 yards—Sammy Baugh, Washington Redskins

Highest Average, Season
51.3 yards—Sammy Baugh, Washington Redskins (1940)

ALL-TIME DROP-KICKING RECORDS

Most Field Goals, Game
4—Paddy Driscoll, Chicago Cardinals vs. Columbus Tigers, October 11, 1925

Longest Field Goal
50 yards—Paddy Driscoll, Chicago Cardinals vs. Milwaukee Badgers, September 28, 1924; Chicago Cardinals vs. Columbus Tigers, October 11, 1925
50 yards—Wilbur Henry, Canton Bulldogs vs. Toledo Maroons, November 13, 1922

STATISTICAL CHAMPIONS—FIELD GOALS

(Players listed represent teams of the National Football League unless noted otherwise.)

1932	Earl Clark, Portsmouth Spartans	3
1933	Jack Manders, Chicago Bears	6
	Glen Presnell, Portsmouth Spartans	6
1934	Jack Manders, Chicago Bears	10
1935	Armand Niccolai, Pittsburgh Steelers	6
	Bill Smith, Chicago Cardinals	6

1936	Jack Manders, Chicago Bears	7
	Armand Niccolai, Pittsburgh Steelers	7
1937	Jack Manders, Chicago Bears	8
1938	Ward Cuff, New York Giants	5
	Ralph Kercheval, Brooklyn Dodgers	5
1939	Ward Cuff, New York Giants	7
1940	Clarke Hinkle, Green Bay Packers	9
1941	Clarke Hinkle, Green Bay Packers	6
1942	Bill Daddio, Chicago Cardinals	5
1943	Ward Cuff, New York Giants	3
	Don Hutson, Green Bay Packers	3
1944	Ken Strong, New York Giants	6
1945	Joe Aguirre, Washington Redskins	7
1946	Ted Fritsch, Green Bay Packers	9
	Lou Groza, Cleveland Browns (AAFC)	13
1947	Ward Cuff, Green Bay Packers	7
	Pat Harder, Chicago Cardinals	7
	Bob Waterfield, Los Angeles Rams	7
	Ben Agajanian, Los Angeles Dons (AAFC)	15
1948	Cliff Patton, Philadelphia Eagles	8
	Rex Grossman, Baltimore Colts (AAFC)	10
1949	Cliff Patton, Philadelphia Eagles	9
	Bob Waterfield, Los Angeles Rams	9
	Howard Johnson, New York Yankees (AAFC)	7
1950	Lou Groza, Cleveland Browns	13
1951	Bob Waterfield, Los Angeles Rams	13
1952	Lou Groza, Cleveland Browns	19
1953	Lou Groza, Cleveland Browns	23
1954	Lou Groza, Cleveland Browns	16
1955	Fred Cone, Green Bay Packers	16
1956	Sam Baker, Washington Redskins	17
1957	Lou Groza, Cleveland Browns	15

1958	Paige Cothren, Los Angeles Rams	14
	Tom Miner, Pittsburgh Steelers	14
1959	Pat Summerall, New York Giants	20
1960	Tommy Davis, San Francisco 49ers	19
	Gene Mingo, Denver Broncos (AFL)	18
1961	Steve Myhra, Baltimore Colts	21
	Gino Cappelletti, Boston Patriots (AFL)	17
1962	Gene Mingo, Denver Broncos (AFL)	27
	Lou Michaels, Pittsburgh Steelers	26
1963	Jim Martin, Baltimore Colts	24
	Gino Cappelletti, Boston Patriots (AFL)	22
1964	Jim Bakken, St. Louis Cardinals	25
	Gino Cappelletti, Boston Patriots (AFL)	25
1965	Pete Gogolak, Buffalo Bills (AFL)	28
	Fred Cox, Minnesota Vikings	23
1966	Bruce Gossett, Los Angeles Rams	28
	Mike Mercer, Kansas City Chiefs (AFL)	21
1967	Jim Bakken, St. Louis Cardinals	27
	Jan Stenerud, Kansas City Chiefs (AFL)	21
1968	Jim Turner, New York Jets (AFL)	34
	Mac Percival, Chicago Bears	25
1969	Jim Turner, New York Jets (AFL)	32
	Fred Cox, Minnesota Vikings (NFC)	26
1970	Fred Cox, Minnesota Vikings (NFC)	30
	Jan Stenerud, Kansas City Chiefs (AFC)	30
1971	Curt Knight, Washington Redskins (NFC)	29
	Garo Yepremian, Miami Dolphins (AFC)	28
1972	Chester Marcol, Green Bay Packers (NFC)	33
	Roy Gerela, Pittsburgh Steelers (AFC)	28

STATISTICAL CHAMPIONS — PUNTING

(Players listed represent teams of the National Football League unless noted otherwise.

		Number of Attempts	Average Yards Per Punt
1939	Parker Hall, Cleveland Rams	58	40.8
1940	Sammy Baugh, Washington Redskins	35	51.4
1941	Sammy Baugh, Washington Redskins	30	48.7
1942	Sammy Baugh, Washington Redskins	37	48.2
1943	Sammy Baugh, Washington Redskins	50	45.9
1944	Frank Sinkwich, Detroit Lions	45	41.0
1945	Roy McKay, Green Bay Packers	44	41.2
1946	Roy McKay, Green Bay Packers	64	42.7
	Glenn Dobbs, Brooklyn Dodgers (AAFC)	80	47.8
1947	Jack Jacobs, Green Bay Packers	57	43.5
	John Colmer, Brooklyn Dodgers (AAFC)	56	44.7
1948	Joe Muha, Philadelphia Eagles	57	47.3
	Glenn Dobbs, Los Angeles Dons (AAFC)	68	49.1
1949	Mike Boyda, New York Bulldogs	56	44.2
1950	Fred Morrison, Chicago Bears	57	43.3
1951	Horace Gillom, Cleveland Browns	73	45.5
1952	Horace Gillom, Cleveland Browns	61	45.7
1953	Pat Brady, Pittsburgh Steelers	80	46.9
1954	Pat Brady, Pittsburgh Steelers	66	43.2
1955	Norm Van Brocklin, Los Angeles Rams	60	44.6
1956	Norm Van Brocklin, Los Angeles Rams	48	43.1
1957	Don Chandler, New York Giants	60	44.6
1958	Sam Baker, Washington Redskins	48	45.4
1959	Yale Lary, Detroit Lions	45	47.1

1960	Jerry Norton, St. Louis Cardinals	39	45.6
	Paul Maguire, Los Angeles Chargers (AFL)	43	40.5
1961	Yale Lary, Detroit Lions	52	48.4
	Billy Atkins, Buffalo Bills (AFL)	85	44.5
1962	Tommy Davis, San Francisco 49ers	48	45.6
	Jim Fraser, Denver Broncos (AFL)	55	43.6
1963	Yale Lary, Detroit Lions	35	48.9
	Jim Fraser, Denver Broncos (AFL)	81	44.4
1964	Bobby Walden, Minnesota Vikings	72	46.4
	Jim Fraser, Denver Broncos (AFL)	73	44.2
1965	Gary Collins, Cleveland Browns	65	46.7
	Jerrel Wilson, Kansas City Chiefs (AFL)	69	45.4
1966	Bob Scarpitto, Denver Broncos (AFL)	76	45.8
	David Lee, Baltimore Colts	49	45.6
1967	Bob Scarpitto, Denver Broncos (AFL)	105	44.9
	Billy Lothridge, Atlanta Falcons	87	43.7
1968	Jerrel Wilson, Kansas City Chiefs (AFL)	63	45.1
	Billy Lothridge, Atlanta Falcons	75	44.3
1969	David Lee, Baltimore Colts	57	45.3
	Dennis Partee, San Diego Chargers (AFL)	71	44.6
1970	Dave Lewis, Cincinnati Bengals (AFC)	79	46.2
	Julian Fagan, New Orleans Saints (NFC)	77	42.5
1971	Dave Lewis, Cincinnati Bengals (AFC)	72	44.8
	Tom McNeill, Philadelphia Eagles (NFC)	73	42.0
1972	Jerrel Wilson, Kansas City Chiefs (AFC)	66	44.8
	Dave Chapple, Los Angeles Rams (NFC)	53	44.2

(Key to abbreviations: AFC, American Football Conference, National Football League; NFC, National Football Conference, National Football League; AFL, American Football League; AAFC, All-America Football Conference)

INDEX

142

143

Running game, 59, 76, 112, 125
Rutgers University, 11
Ruth, Babe, 53

Saban, Lou, 65, 66
St. Louis Cardinals, 39, 50, 138, 139, 141
St. Nicholas magazine, 132
San Diego Chargers, 27, 33, 56, 58, 70, 98, 141
Sayers, Gale, 107, 109, 110
Scarpitto, Bob, 141
Seaver, Tom, 10
Seiple, Larry, 124
Shula, Don, 79
Simpson, O. J., 129
Smith, Bill, 137
Smith, Bubba, 117
Snap-back, 12, 47, 48, 49, 50
Spalding, A. G., Company, 22
Sport magazine, 58
Sporting News, 30
Staten Island Stapletons, 21, 22
Stroud, Morris, 119, 120
Studstill, Pat, 124
Summerall, Pat, 138
Super Bowl, 10, 47, 74, 75, 83, 120

Tackle, 26, 29, 33, 64, 101, 132
Tarkenton, Fran, 46, 81
Team rosters, 24
Thompson, Rocky, 103
Thompson, Tommy, 24
Thorpe, Jim, 13, 14, 15, 16, 17, 132, 133
Tingelhoff, Mick, 48
Tittle, Y. A., 52
Toledo Maroons, 132, 136
Touchdown passes, 13, 18, 29, 30, 52, 53, 54, 57, 63
Training camp, 53, 56, 65, 82, 87, 97
Turner, Jim, 51, 68, 83, 84, 129, 130, 135, 139

U. S. Indian Industrial School, 13
University of Chicago, 100
University of Florida, 95
University of Indiana, 78
University of Indianapolis, 78
University of Kentucky, 53
University of Minnesota, 19, 65
University of New Mexico, 26
University of Notre Dame, 17
University of Oklahoma, 95

University of Pittsburgh, 81

Van Brocklin, Norm, 79, 140
Volk, Rick, 114

Walden, Bob, 141
Walker, Mike, 35
Walsh, Bill, 97
Walter Camp's All American team, 100
Ward, John, 123
Warner, Glen S. (Pop), 18
Washington Redskins, 18, 19, 45, 47, 87, 127, 136, 137, 138, 139, 140
Waterfield, Bob, 23, 62, 67, 137, 138
Wells, Warren, 58
Widby, Ron, 86, 89
Williams, Travis, 109, 110
Wilson, Jerrel, 85, 86, 93, 95, 98, 126, 141
Wilson, Larry, 50
Wood, Gary, 46

Yepremian, Garo, 10, 36, 45, 76, 77, 78, 79, 139